"What a great book! *Loving God When You Don't Love the Church* is an amazing exposé that addresses critical issues of our day with wisdom instead of sarcasm, with truths that heal and with love that confronts. For once we have a book that speaks truth with grace. I applaud the valiant efforts of Chris Jackson!"

Dr. James W. Goll, Encounters Network; author,
The Seer, The Coming Prophetic Revolution,
The Lost Art of Intercession and many more

"I can assure you that you will experience the heart of God through the pages of this book. You will feel the Lord's love and passion emanating from each page and be refreshed in your personal relationship with Him. Healing will come to your soul in the places where you have been wounded by the Church. You will receive a fresh anointing and the understanding and commissioning to *be* the Church in the 21st century."

Dutch Sheets, senior pastor, Freedom Church

"Our generation is filled with those who love the Gospel but hate the Church, who cling to Jesus but who can barely tolerate His Bride. The wounds and the bitterness are killing our life in God. Chris Jackson shows us a path to healing by showing us the biblical path to Christlike character. How desperately we need what this rising voice has to say!"

Stephen Mansfield, The Mansfield Group

"What a timely message for the Christian Church! This book provides words of healing and perspective for those who have been wounded or who have become disillusioned with the Church, and it builds a bridge of understanding for both leaders and laity. Read it and pass it on. Someone you know needs this book."

Stan Fleming, Gatebreaker Ministries

LOVING
GOD
WHEN YOU
DON'T LOVE
THE
CHURCH

OPENING THE
DOOR TO HEALING

CHRIS JACKSON

Chosen
Grand Rapids, Michigan

Published by Chosen Books
A division of Baker Publishing Group
P.O. Box 6287, Grand Rapids, MI 49516-6287
www.chosenbooks.com

Second printing, December 2007

Printed in the United States of America

Library of Congress Cataloging-in-Publication Data
Jackson, Chris, 1972–
    Loving God when you don't love the church : opening the door to heal-
ing / Chris Jackson.
        p.   cm.
    Includes bibliographical references.
    ISBN 10: 0-8007-9431-1 (pbk.)
    ISBN 978-0-8007-9431-6 (pbk.)
    1. Church membership. 2. Ex-church members. 3. Reconciliation—
Religious aspects—Christianity. 4. Religious addiction—Christianity.
5. Psychology, Religious. I. Title.
BV820.J33 2007
248.8′6—dc22   2007009667

For Jessica,
The North Atlantic

Contents

FOREWORD

I believe with all my heart that God's passion is to pour out His Spirit all over the world. I believe He is coming to all the nations of the earth with the unstoppable force of His power and unconditional love. And I believe He is coming to *you*.

For the Lord to have His way on the earth and to establish the fullness of His Kingdom as He desires, He must have a Church who looks like Him and is able to work with Him to overthrow hell and conquer territory for His glory. He will have a healthy Bride who is prepared and ready to obey His commands.

Unfortunately, many people in His Church have been isolated and wounded—not just through the firepower of the enemy but from "friendly fire" within the Church herself. And the Church of Jesus Christ today is often *not* a bastion of love, healing and Christlikeness but of pride, performance and lifeless religious activity.

In His quest to revive the world, the Lord wants to start with His Church. He wants to heal and restore her and bring her back to her primary calling of looking like Him and making Him famous in the world. He is looking for sons and daughters who will displace hell and bear His image with passion and excellence in every sector of society.

I have had the privilege of mentoring and serving with Chris Jackson, and I can assure you that you will experience the heart of God through the pages of this book. You will feel the Lord's love and passion emanating from each page and be refreshed in your personal relationship with Him. Healing will come to your soul in the places where you have been wounded by the Church. You will receive a fresh anointing and the understanding and commissioning to *be* the Church in the 21st century.

So please, journey on and experience on a personal level the inescapable promise of Jesus from Matthew 16:18: "I will build My church; and the gates of Hades will not overpower it." He is building *you* and He loves you, and nothing will stop His plan in your life!

Dutch Sheets, senior pastor, Freedom Church; president, Dutch Sheets Ministries, Colorado Springs, Colorado

1

HAVE YOU EVER BEEN HURT IN THE CHURCH?

Two roads diverged in a wood, and I,
I took the road less traveled by,
And that has made all the difference.

Robert Frost

You're reaping the consequences of your sinful life."
He broke her heart that day, and she's still recovering from it.

He was a pastor, and she went to him expecting to catch a glimpse of Jesus, but instead she was judged. She called me recently from another state and told me that no matter how hard she prays, she can't feel clean.

I did my best to tell her that Jesus specializes in *removing* our sinful pasts. I shared with her how the word *mercy* in Scripture literally means a compassion that *alleviates* the hurtful consequences of wrong decisions. I tried to tell her that God loves her and that there are churches out there that will accept her and love her for who she really is—a beautiful daughter of the King.

Unfortunately, the church has already told her otherwise.

Oh, how I wish hers was an isolated incident. I wish you were shocked to read about it. I wish you had never even heard about the experience of this woman. Realistically, though, I know that you, too, have heard your share of horror stories like hers. I'm sure you know this woman. In fact, you may even be *like* this woman.

I know that I am.

Many of us are.

We are the woman at the well. We're looking for life. We're carrying a thirst that can't be satisfied. We know that we were destined for more than the way we're living, so we set out in search of real life. We go to the only place we know to try to draw living water.

We go to church.

What do we find there? Not what we expected.

I have mixed feelings as I write this because I've seen so many contradictory things in church, and I've *experienced* so many contradictory things in church. I love the church—but I hate certain parts of it. I adore the people of God—but I've also been hurt so deeply by some of them that I almost lost my faith. In church I've met some of the sweetest saints to ever grace the planet—but I've also been lied about and slandered behind my back.

I've experienced true, covenant friendship in the church—but I've also experienced Judas' kiss in the church. I've encountered God in the church—but I've also been nearly killed by religion. I've tasted the presence that's brought me life—but I've also been suffocated by legalism and control. I love God. But for a while I wanted to say "forget the church."

I met my wife in church. My children were dedicated to God in church. The greatest and most loyal friendships

I've ever known were formed in church. I discovered my calling in church. Throughout history, the Church has been one of the greatest agents of mercy that the world has ever seen. The Church is the Bride of Christ, and He loves her passionately! I love her, too.

Thus, my mixed feelings.

For as wonderful as she is, the Body of Christ is filled with wounded sons and daughters who came to church looking for life, but were disappointed. Instead, they encountered a religious system that left them lying on the road to Jericho right beside the man in Jesus' story. Instead of meeting Good Samaritans who would tend their wounds and bear their burdens, they were left to bleed as pious worshipers looked the other way.

Am I being overly dramatic and critical? I probably am. I know that there are incredible people in church who lay their lives down for hurting humanity. It's just that I, too, have lain in the ditch of despair, and I was shocked to see that hundreds and thousands of Christians were lying there beside me.

But just as I am about to point my own righteous finger at this hypocritical element in the church, it dawns on me. *I am the Church.*

I have been hypocritical and judgmental. *I've* lived in a spiritual frat house. *I've* overlooked the gifts and potential of precious saints because I couldn't see past their baggage. *I've* been unloving. *I've* been controlling. *I've* looked like anything but Christ.

Some of those disillusioned ones lying in the ditch were helped there *by me.*

Not all of them have left the church, of course. Many of them still worship beside us every Sunday morning. They love God, and they are still committed to His plan for their lives; incidentally, so are many of the ones who no longer attend corporate church services.

They're awesome people! They could be some of the greatest leaders the Church has ever seen. It's just that they've been wounded and rejected, and their hearts are carrying some burning questions: *Where is the Church that Jesus said He would build? Where can I find the abundant life that He talked about? Where can I fit in and find real, unforced relationships? Where is the living water that my soul so desperately craves? And, possibly most important of all, why do church wounds go so deep and take so long to heal?*

I want to process these and other questions with you, and I also want to heal with you. Let's journey together through our histories and our hurts, and let's experience the unconditional love of God. Let's explore our mountaintops and our valleys, and let's rediscover the wonder of Christian spirituality, the beauty of the Church and the indispensable role that God has fashioned for each of us to play.

He loves you. He's longing for you. *You* are the Church. *You* are the apple of His eye, and He is pursuing you with the passion of a desperate lover. *He is not the church that hurt you!*

If you genuinely love the Lord and yet today, due to hurts from a church, find yourself disillusioned or struggling to retain the wonder of your initial encounter with God, this book is for you. This book is designed to mend your brokenness, restretch your sails and fill you with the love and the breath of God again.

If you have experienced betrayal or rejection in a church, this book is for you.

If you genuinely love God but wrestle to find healing from wounds that occurred—not on some spiritual battlefield, but within the walls of your own local congregation—this book is for you.

If you took your thirst to church but left even more parched and dry . . .

If you're still hungering for an elusive abundant life . . .

If, despite your negative experiences, you realize that *you are called to be the Church* . . .

If you've lost some hope along the way but *you still have a desire to make your life count for the Kingdom of God* . . .

If *you long to take your place as a powerful 21*st*-century Christian of impact* . . .

. . . this is your story!

We are in the most critical hour of world history, as light and dark and good and evil converge with greater force than in any other era. Multiple kingdoms are clashing all around us with horrific strength and violence. If there were ever an hour for the Church to be the Church, it is now. The world is waiting in the wings, and *it needs you*. It needs me, too.

Two roads have diverged in the woods of our lives. One path leads to healing, forgiveness and a fresh encounter with the One who loves us most. The other leads to increasing places of hurt and rejection that will ultimately quench our love and derail our destinies. The first path requires courage, honesty, humility, grace and a willingness to move on. The second requires nothing at all.

Let's embrace the more difficult road. Let's journey together for a little while and receive the healing and refreshing of God. Let's recapture the wonder of His Kingdom, and let's assume our role in His epic story.

Let's embrace the road less traveled and become His answer for the world.

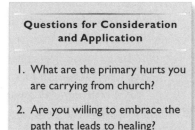

Questions for Consideration and Application

1. What are the primary hurts you are carrying from church?

2. Are you willing to embrace the path that leads to healing?

2

The Left Behind

Heavy the sorrow that bows the head,
When love is alive and hope is dead.

W. S. Gilbert

Man's extremity is God's opportunity.

John Flavel

Don't you love reunions? Once the initial nervousness passes, it's delightful to catch up on all the news. What's the latest in your world? How is so-and-so? Did you hear she got married? Did you know they moved to Europe? My sister finally had her baby! It's great to reconnect with those significant relationships from our past.

At least, it usually is.

I was visiting with a friend from my hometown a few years back, and as we got caught up on all the juicy news, I asked what I thought would be a simple, innocent question. Boy, was I ever wrong. We had a mutual friend whom I hadn't seen in some time, so I asked, "How is he doing?"

My friend's eyebrows furrowed, and his hands tightly clenched the steering wheel of his car. He sighed in disgust and said, "I feel sorry for his kids."

"Why?" I asked, curious and a little bit alarmed.

"I just can't believe what he's teaching them and modeling for them."

"What is he teaching them?" I asked with a mounting dread, fearing that my old acquaintance had either committed some foul sin or embraced some heretical doctrine.

"He's teaching them that it's okay to be a covenant breaker."

"What do you mean? How did he break covenant? Did he have an affair? Did he divorce his wife?"

My friend was silent for a moment as he considered the best way to break the terrible news to me. "No," he said slowly. "He left the church. He disagreed with the leadership about some things and decided to move on. Now his children are being taught that it's okay to break covenant and bail out when things don't go their way."

I didn't know how to respond to him as a surge of strong emotions grew inside me. I finally asked, "Have you spoken with him about his decision? Do you know what his perspective is? Do you know how he's doing?"

My friend replied a little too quickly. "No—I don't think I could be around him right now. It would be too awkward to associate with him, plus I'm afraid for him since he's in such a bad place."

At that point, the reunion soured for me. I just wanted to get out of the car and skip the rest of the catching up. I felt angry and grieved, and I wondered why it is that we Christians can be so quick to write people off when they make decisions with which we disagree.

I don't know if my friend was right or not. Maybe a relational covenant *had* been broken. Maybe our mutual friend *did* handle his situation foolishly, and maybe he *was* leading his family in a dangerous direction. I don't know the answers to these questions, but I do know that I have seen many "concerned" believers pass harsh judgment on their fellow Christians who disagree with them or who choose to move in a different direction.

I am the pastor of a local church, and *I hate it when people leave my church*. I wish that every guest who visited my church would fall in love with us and never want to leave. I wish they would experience God, make lifelong friendships, receive training in the area of their giftedness and make an impact *with us* for the Kingdom of God. I hate the "Pastor, God is moving us on" talks. Sometimes I can understand why people want to leave our church, and sometimes I completely disagree with their rationale. Sometimes I feel worried or angry, and sometimes I just want to cry for hours.

I don't believe, however, that if people leave my church, or disagree with me over a particular point of view, that they are committing a sin equivalent to cheating on their spouse or violating the Ten Commandments. Even if I hate their choice to leave, I don't believe they should be treated like a social leper and be avoided in the aisles of the grocery store.

That happens, you know.

I hope you don't think I'm overstating my case—I've seen these and other comparable actions many times in my own life. I've seen people be completely rejected when they *appropriately* questioned church leadership. I've heard people be harshly judged by pastors and parishioners alike after leaving a congregation. I've seen many people left behind as soon as they disagreed with something in their church, and I think it breaks God's heart. I think we're too quick to leave people behind.

I realize, of course, that there are times when we need to challenge rebellious behavior, and there are times when we need to admonish and question decisions and courses of action, but those times aren't what I'm concerned about here. I'm concerned about those who are left behind. I'm concerned about those who came to churches looking for life and instead left with a formula. I'm concerned about those who dropped their guard and received a punch in the gut while in the house of the Lord. I'm concerned about those who perhaps *did* make some mistakes but received the death sentence for a misdemeanor. I'm concerned *about you*.

What happens after people get left behind? Where do they go? Where are they now?

According to research from respected church historian George Barna, they're everywhere. Some are still in churches, dutifully attending services each week; others are at home watching football. Some are experiencing more fellowship in the local pub than they *ever* experienced in the local church; some are in full-time church work. They are you. And they are me.

We've been left behind.

No, I don't mean *left behind* in the Tim LaHaye sense of the term. I mean that we have experienced the unraveling of significant church relationships, and we've been struggling to find closure and peace ever since. We're not obsessive, and we're not intentionally unforgiving or bitter—we're just confused. What went wrong? Why did things have to end this way? Aren't we supposed to be the Body of Christ? I was trained to be on guard against *the devil*—I never expected to be taken out by *friendly fire*.

And yet the fire came.

I guess I'm okay with disagreements—to a degree. I remember that even David had to dodge a few spears in the house of the king of Israel, so I understand that sometimes painful things *do* happen in the family of Christ. I realize that the Lord may use the weaknesses in those around me to shape and mold *my* character—it's just that when it happened, I didn't expect it and it didn't make any sense. It still doesn't.

I feel left behind—and it's hard to get over it. No matter how I try, I can't stop processing it. In fact, I did it again just last night.

I promised myself I wouldn't, and I *almost* made it. For a while, I kept my vow. I bit my tongue. I tried to talk about other things. I dodged it and I avoided it, and then it just tumbled out. "What do you think happened?"

Jessica and I were eating dinner with some precious friends who have acted as spiritual mentors in our lives when I asked the question. I couldn't help it. We were discussing our families and the blessings of God, but I couldn't escape my inner turmoil over some unresolved issues. I needed some outside help and perspective as to why some of the relationships that I had prized and esteemed in my church had unraveled so badly.

They weren't just interpersonal relationships that involved me—they were much bigger than me. They involved church-philosophy issues and relationships between spiritual leaders that disintegrated and, in the fallout, damaged hundreds of lives.

"Do you know what went wrong? Did you ever have any conversations about it? Were you ever alarmed by it?" My friends had some great perspectives that helped me a lot and enabled me to view certain situations through a bigger picture grid than I had possessed before. It was wonderful to speak with them, and I experienced a measure of healing from our time together. As we left, though, I wondered why I *still* felt such a strong desire to talk about the past. I wondered why it always came up in conversation and why I couldn't bite my tongue a little harder.

I think the answer is relatively simple. It's not that I really didn't understand the situation or that I couldn't articulate what happened—I knew what went wrong. I knew why things had unraveled. That's not what kept me up at night.

That's not why I brought it up in every conversation I had with people who were related to the situation. I realized that evening that the reason I was so plagued with frustration and hurt was that before that specific night, *I had never been heard.*

The heart cry of justice is a longing to be heard!

I had finally been heard—and some healing had finally made its way into my soul.

I needed to be healed. In some ways, I was like the fellow in Jesus' story of the Good Samaritan. Do you remember that story? Most kids who have ever been in Sunday school do.

It's the story of four men: the wounded traveler (the one who was left behind), the priest (the church leader), the Levite (the church member) and the Samaritan (the unchurched man who most resembled Jesus in the story). The Good Samaritan understandably steals the spotlight because he was the only one to demonstrate kindness and because Jesus pointed to him as a role model of Christian charity. However, he wasn't the primary character in the story. The only man who can be found in the entire story—from the opening scene to the ending credits—was the wounded man who had been left behind on the side of the road.

We all aspire to be like the Good Samaritan, and we all shake our heads as we vow never to be like the priest or the Levite, but what we sometimes miss is that in certain parts of our lives, we aren't any of those men—we're the poor bloke who has been beaten and left for dead on the road to Jericho. We need a Samaritan. And in our need *for* him, we vow to *be* him.

I don't just want to be a Good Samaritan because he was a great guy whom Jesus commended in the story. I want to be a Good Samaritan because *I've lain in the road while priests and Levites have passed me by.* I've seen them look the other way, and it has bothered me so deeply that, years later while eating with friends, I'm still asking, "What do you think went wrong?"

I've needed a Good Samaritan. Thank God, I've found him in Jesus! Thank God I've found him in dozens of amazing people who rushed to my side, bandaged my wounds, set me on their donkey, took me to the inn and paid my expenses when I was too out of it to function. I love the Good Samaritan! I want to be him. Because I know what it feels like to lie on the side of the road, and because I know what it's like to be set back on my feet, I want to spend my life helping others do the same. I realize that not everyone has experienced the strong arms of the Good Samaritan the way I have—many people are still lying there, stinging from their rejection by the Levite.

I think they're waiting for me. I think they're waiting for *you*.

The conclusion of Jesus' story charges us with the words, "Go and do the same" (Luke 10:37).

I can hear Him speaking still:

"Go and rescue My people who have been battered by the cares of life!

"Go and displace hell wherever it has reared its ugly head!

"Allow your own need for mercy to make you *a vessel of mercy* that pours My love into the world."

Questions for Consideration and Application

1. Do you still have hurts from areas where you were never heard?

2. If so, do you need to process those hurts with someone who can help?

3. Even if you currently feel like the wounded man in Jesus' story, are you willing to be the Good Samaritan for someone else who has been wounded like you?

3

CHURCH WOUNDS

Afflictions are but the shadows of God's wings.
George Macdonald

Earth has no sorrow that heaven cannot heal.
Thomas Moore

P lease forgive us in advance!" I always say this at the
beginning of our church's new members' classes. As I
look into the beautiful eyes of the excited, hopeful people
(sons and daughters, fathers and mothers, with unique and
wonderful stories of their own), I cringe to think that some of
them won't experience what they are hoping to experience
with us. I silently ask the Lord for mercy and to cover our
church's glaring humanity. I know these people are joining
our congregation because they believe the Lord has planted
them there and because they expect to grow and experience
God during their tenure with us. They're looking for life, and
I hope very much that we don't disappoint them.

Unfortunately, I know we will.

We're human, after all. So are you. And so is every church
on the face of the planet. That's the problem—people bring
their heart's desires and spiritual longings into churches full

of very *human* beings who, although they are trying their best to love and obey God, will very possibly be used by either God or the devil to wound and maim their souls. If God is behind the wounding, it is for the purpose of stimulating growth, maturity and a greater dependence on Him. If it is the devil at work, it is for the purpose of destroying faith and giving a black eye to the church.

Sadly, in many instances, churches are wearing sunglasses to hide the marks of the devil in their midst. I've got a nice, dark pair myself.

So in our new members' classes, as we embark on a new relationship as fellow church members, I appeal to them to walk in love and in the light. I assure them that if we do indeed hurt them, we will be committed to humility and reconciliation. With as much fervency as I can muster, I assure them that we will try our best to serve their calling and their families and be a safe place for them to grow and experience the wonder and mystery of life in Christ. With all my heart, I hope we live up to those promises.

I remind them of one of my favorite thoughts: "God doesn't wound us in our bald spots." This comes from Psalm 68:21, in which David wrote that God wounds "the hairy crown of him who goes on in his guilty deeds." I love that verse! He wounds us in our *hairy heads*—He doesn't expose us and embarrass us in our most vulnerable areas. Rather, He loves us and wants to cover us, and He wants His Church to do the same.

Part of my problem is that I've experienced the opposite in church. I've been "beaten in my bald spot," and I can show you the scars to prove it. One thing I've learned during my lifetime in church is that *church wounds go incredibly deep and they take a very long time to heal.*

Why is that? Why is it that people who have been wounded in a church will still be talking about their wounds years later? Why can people forgive a betraying friend or experience a business meltdown and move on with life, but if it is a church that fails them, it is nearly impossible to let it go? Have you ever seen this dynamic in others? Have you ever lived it yourself?

I've experienced this in my personal life, and I've observed it in the lives of hundreds of others. There are hurts that I received in church over a decade ago that *I'm still talking about*. I know people who have taken a beating in church and, although I have deep compassion for them, I get a little nervous when I see them because I know they will criticize the church throughout our entire visit.

I've seen friendships form around the common denominator of anger toward a particular church or church leader. Before the hurt these people were virtual strangers, but they suddenly find each other as long lost brothers or sisters and build an entire relationship on the foundation of their mutual hurt and disappointment with the church that hurt them.

Some local churches get planted out of a reaction to prior negative church experiences. I've heard of small-group gatherings that spend more time railing on their former (or current) church than they do worshiping Jesus and challenging one another to grow. When wounded Christians get together, it seems that they inevitably turn to criticizing the church that hurt them.

I wonder why we do this. I wonder why we can't just let it go. I wonder why it is so difficult for us to forgive our church leaders and our church friends and just carry on with life. Why do we keep reliving past issues? Is it healthy? Is it therapeutic? Does it help to bring closure and a fresh beginning?

The answer is *no*! No, it is never healthy to gossip and criticize. No, it doesn't bring healing and closure to constantly regurgitate an offense. It never glorifies Jesus to backstab and to complain.

I think I know why we do it, though.

I'm convinced that church wounds are especially painful and run a little deeper than other hurts because they catch us completely off guard. *We don't expect to get hurt in church.* Because the Church is supposed to be a place of healing and acceptance, no one expects to get shot while there.

Dr. Martin Luther King Jr. rightly said that we should preach a "whosoever will, let him come" gospel. People appropriately expect that they will experience this "whosoever will, let him come" mentality in church. They believe that they will be loved and accepted when they show up for a service. They expect to get a holy kiss, but when they get one from Judas instead, it surprises them, and the force of the blow is extra deadly.

In boxing, they say that it's the punch you don't see coming that will take you out. A good boxer can weather the most brutal of punches if he sees it coming. The unseen blow, however, is the one that will send any fighter to the canvas. Church blows are unseen blows. People come to worship—and they don't expect to take a shot in the gut.

I watched Oscar De La Hoya get knocked out recently by Bernard Hopkins. I am a die-hard De La Hoya fan, and I was shocked as a quick shot to the gut dropped the Golden Boy to the canvas, where he sprawled for the count. Another thirty seconds and he would have been fully recovered to continue the bout, but the unseen blow to the gut took him out and ended his dramatic ascent through the middle-weight classes. I'm certainly no De La Hoya, but I, too, recently received a surprise shot that momentarily stunned me.

It came from my four-year-old daughter, who placed a well-aimed kick in my solar plexus the other day. We were wrestling, and as she tried to squirm away, she launched her blow to my unsuspecting midsection. For a brief second it took my breath away—*and she's only four.* How much more painful when the kick comes from "my companion and my familiar friend; we who had sweet fellowship together" (Psalm 55:13–14)?

People don't expect to get hurt in church, so when they do, the piercing pain runs especially deep.

Not only are people unprepared for church hurts, but when the wounds come, they often never receive closure. People don't expect to be wounded in the house of their brothers and sisters in the first place, and then, once they receive the hurt, they very likely are never met by the leadership with a humble embrace and a desire to pursue reconciliation. *They are never heard.*

As I said in the last chapter, *the heart cry of justice is a longing to be heard.* Sometimes people don't even want a favorable verdict as much as they want a fair hearing. Because God is a God of justice, there is an innate longing for this justice in the heart of every human being. When justice is perceived to be thwarted, people will find an audience somewhere to listen to their case.

Sometimes we slander the church that hurt us to whoever will listen, simply because the church won't hear us. I'm not blaming these churches entirely. I know that sometimes people overreact and resist the legitimate correction of the Lord in their lives; however, I'm not sure that this is true in the majority of cases. I think there are often good people with legitimate questions and concerns who never received a fair hearing in church. They get hurt, and then either they or the church (or both) fail to respond properly to the offense. The wounded party eventually ends up in the aisle of a grocery store telling anyone who will listen about the vices of their former church or pastor.

I don't think people come to this place because they are bad people. I think they get driven there by their hurt. Church wounds go deeper than some people realize because they are unexpected wounds and often there is not an accompanying experience of closure. The wounded wonder, *How can I fully heal if there is no closure, no hope of reconciliation and no ownership of the wrong?* It's a fair question that often doesn't get answered.

Another reason that church wounds go especially deep and take extra time to heal is that *church wounds usually occur in vulnerable places*.

A good church service pulls the vulnerability out of people. When God's presence is strong in a corporate worship setting, hopefully people will drop their guard and invite Him in. When a sermon is anointed and passionate, people will open their hearts to the words and the message behind it. People come to church expecting to find answers and help for the tender spots in their lives. Corporate church gatherings tout an ability to meet the vulnerable heart cry of passersby, so people come and bring their vulnerability to Jesus.

They're looking for *Him*, you know. They are looking for healing, and they are looking to be trained in the area of their destinies (usually the most personal part of their hearts). They are looking for relationships, and they are often taking risks in all of these areas; consequently, they end up stretched out and exposed. That's not a bad position to be in, they think, because, after all, they are in the house of God. If they are ever going to be vulnerable and real, it should be there.

That stretched-out position, though, is a very delicate one.

My dad broke a rib once because he dove onto the sand in a stretched-out position. At the time, we were creating one of my favorite childhood memories. We had been surfing at Huntington Beach in California, and after we finished, Dad began chasing me down the beach with a handful of melted

M&Ms. In a desperate effort to catch me and anoint me with chocolate, he dove—fully extended—toward my fleeing form. In that stretched-out position, he landed directly on his exposed ribcage and spent the rest of our vacation nursing a bruised side and a broken rib.

We stretch ourselves in church. We stretch ourselves in ministry, in relationships and in faith, and if there's no one to catch us when we trip, we can crack and break.

There are many wonderful Christians out there (like you) who have been broken in the house of the Lord. It's a tragedy to think that they're carrying unheard grievances and disappointments. Some of the grievances are justified. Some are rooted in rebellion. Others are laced with deception. But all of them are carried by people who are loved by God and who have a right to be heard.

Even if an irreconcilable difference causes a rift between a person and his or her church (or church leadership), there are still scriptural precedents for how *both parties* should respond. If the church were more biblical in its approach to its people, church wounds would be less frequent, would pierce less deeply and wouldn't take so long to heal.

Sometimes, instead of being like Jesus, churches look more like one of my favorite westerns: Clint Eastwood's *The Good, the Bad and the Ugly*. I like all of the old spaghetti westerns, but there's something about this one that has always fascinated me. I love the gun battles and the music and the rough, gritty reality of life in that era of filmmaking. There are no spotless white hats on the heroes' heads in this movie. In fact, many times throughout the film, it's nearly impossible to discern exactly *who* the heroes are. Sometimes the good looks like the bad, and at different times, *all* of them are ugly.

It's probably a little sacrilegious to compare a church to a Clint Eastwood western, but in some ways it's a fair comparison. The best churches in the world will have things about them that aren't right. The most wonderful congregations will, at times, have an ugly aspect to them. On the other hand, some of the worst churches will contain features that are simply amazing. We all know that there are no perfect churches, but we can all do our part to make our own churches "more perfect" than they currently are. After all, *we*, not the building or the corporation or the organization, are the Church. As we grow into an ever-increasing likeness of Jesus, our churches will grow, too.

There's a frightening little story hidden in the greetings at the end of the apostle Paul's letters that fits very appropriately here at the beginning of our journey together. It centers on a young man named Demas. There's not much written about him in the New Testament, except for the fact that Paul kept telling the brethren at the close of his letters that Demas also sent his love and greetings to them. I don't think I ever would have paid attention to those minor inclusions had I not become fascinated one day with a verse in 2 Timothy written at the very end of Paul's life. While in prison, nearing the end of his life and ministry, Paul expressed to Timothy his heartache over Demas. He said, "Make every effort to come to me soon; for Demas, having loved this present world, has deserted me and gone to Thessalonica" (2 Timothy 4:9–10).

I felt compassion for Paul, who was abandoned at his moment of need at the end of his life, and I began to study each of the references to Demas in the New Testament to try to understand what had happened to him. There are only three or four of these references, but their context reveals quite a lot. Paul considered Demas a friend, a co-worker, a son and a true man of God. As I mused on these descriptions, I realized that Demas was in line to be another Timothy or Titus, and that had things gone differently, we might have had a fourth pastoral epistle in the canon of Scripture called *the book of Demas.*

What happened? How could a spiritual son of the apostle Paul return to the world and abandon the hope of his calling? The answer is actually very simple and very frightening: He experienced the same things you and I have experienced—he was hurt. When Paul said that Demas had *deserted* him and *gone* to Thessalonica, he revealed insight into Demas' story, because the meaning that those words convey is "to turn aside due to piercing or wounding." Paul didn't spell out in black and white what specifically happened to Demas, but the curious, studious reader can deduce that Demas had been pierced, and in the pain of his wounding, he developed a vulnerable spot in his heart. Then one day as he passed through Thessalonica, something caught his eye, triggered the wound and caused him to abandon the faith.

How tragic that a Timothy-in-the-making could be punctured by pain and run away from the Kingdom and back into the arms of the world. How frightening to realize that you and I are also Timothys-in-the-making and that we, too, have been similarly perforated. Let's learn from Demas and commit to live in such a way that if the Bible were still being written today, it just might boast a book that bore *our* names. Let's be Timothys who make every effort to come quickly when the Lord has need of us. Let's take our place in the Body again *and truly become who we really are.*

If Christians like you and me truly acted like the Church, we would have fewer casualties to account for and we might make more progress at satisfying the thirst of our generation. You've noticed how thirsty they are, haven't you? Despite their particular disposition toward church, they're thirsting for God. They're thirsting for a different life, and they expect to find it in church.

**Questions for Consideration
and Application**

1. Are you conducting your spiritual life with a "whosoever will, let him come" doctrine?

2. Have you formed any relationships around the common denominator of hurt and anger toward other Christians?

3. Do you recognize that, like Demas, you could have hurts that are your undoing?

4. Do you know that God believes you can make it?

4

THE OTHER LIFE

*When a man's pursuit gradually makes his face shine
and grow handsome, be sure it is a worthy one.*

William James

The deepest truth blooms only from the deepest love.

Heinrich Heine

*What the heart has once owned and had, it shall never
lose.*

Henry Ward Beecher

There are two lives awaiting you. The first is the life of common sense and sensibility. It is the safe, risk-free life of conventional wisdom and practicality. Many people settle into this vein of living. They go to college. They attend church. They marry. They have children. They retire. And often, they love God.

As wonderful and noble as all of these accomplishments are, they still wrestle with a secret question: *Is there more to life?* Is this the extent of the abundant life I anticipated when I brought my thirst to Jesus?

The Lord will still love you if you choose the ordinary life.

But then there is the other life—*the life that you were meant to live*. The life that has been buried deep inside of you—buried so deep, in fact, that sometimes only an encounter with eternity can awaken it. This is the life that whispers to you in your dreams. This is the life that will ruin you for all other living. This life will break your heart a thousand times and fill you with the inspiration to change the world. It will be a harder life than you ever dreamed you would live, but it will be more beautiful and satisfying than anything you have ever imagined.

This is the life to which God is calling you.

I embraced this call at a moment of extreme desperation during my sophomore year of college.

On Minnehaha

"I'm not leaving until You speak to me! I'm sitting right here until You touch me!"

With these words, I dug my heels in and had it out with God. I was atop a rocky bluff overlooking the Little Spokane River when I settled in for my all-night wrestling match with the Almighty. The mountain was called Minnehaha, a rock climber's paradise, and I had decided that I would meet God there or die trying. I felt like Jacob—desperate, broken and determined that I would not let go until the blessing was mine and I had heard Him call my name.

I prayed for hours. I cried until I was hoarse and breathless and I worshiped like a dying man. And then, finally, I fell asleep. When I awoke, I was sitting on a jagged rock that jutted out from the mountainside and held me precariously above a deadly sixty-foot drop.

Something had changed inside of me. I hadn't seen an angel and I hadn't heard a voice, but I knew my decision was made. As I climbed down the path to the river, I wasn't just walking to my car—I was taking the road less traveled.

And my life would never be the same.

I had climbed Minnehaha the night before, a desperate, imprisoned man—although no one would have known it from the outside. Faithful in my church attendance, enrolled full-time and running track for the local college, holding down a job and pursuing a romantic relationship, I was well along the path that I had set for my life. The problem was that it was the path that *I* had set—and it wasn't the life I was made to live.

The other life had been speaking to me.

I thought it was a new voice, cloaked in the feelings of emptiness that had been growing inside me. I thought it was a new realization that God had other plans for my life than those that I was trying frantically to fulfill. I thought the choking awareness that I was on the wrong path was something new—but I realize now that it had been calling me for a long time.

I probably heard its words most clearly when I was a little boy armed with wooden swords and daggers and assaulting fictitious dragons that guarded hoards of make-believe treasure. I heard it on the riverbanks where I waged, and won, imaginary battles with hideous foes. I caught its message in the movies that stirred my soul, like *Star Wars* and *The Princess Bride*. I tapped into its theme as I wrote countless poems about adventure and romance. I think I heard it most clearly as a child—the other life was beckoning me.

This life has also been beckoning you. Perhaps you have heard it, too, and, like me, you have made a significant life change to accept its invitation.

I quit college and pursued theological training. I laid down work and athletics and relationships, and I lived the Scripture that speaks of Peter's abandoned nets on the seashore. He, too, left the road of safety and dashed down the overgrown path of destiny.

I made a decision to invest in my true calling. I embraced the Lord's plan for my life. It has been exciting and inspiring and glorious—and it has also been more painful than I ever dreamed possible. I wonder why the mysterious voice of destiny never told me I would *lose* some battles. It never told me that I wouldn't always stand atop the dragon, wielding my blood-red sword in victory. Sometimes the dragon gets you—and you have to crawl into a cave to heal for a while.

I don't think it would have mattered even if the voice had given me full disclosure of the risk. We don't care too much about risks when we've had an encounter with eternity and decide to sell out in pursuit of God. All we know is that we were made for Him and that we can't live another day without His presence.

I don't know if your experience was as dramatic as mine (it may have been far *more* dramatic), but you've probably experienced a time when you, too, realized that there was more to life than what you had been living. I'm sure you've faced crossroads in your life where you chose to follow God's leading even if it ran contrary to the conventional wisdom of your well-meaning loved ones. If you have, you've brought heaven to its feet in admiration, you've pleased God and you've embraced the reality that there is another life that bears your name—a life that is found only on God's less-traveled highway. You've probably experienced moments of His pleasure that lifted your spirit higher than the Rocky Mountains and buoyed you during stormy seas. You've probably seen God do some wonderful things on your behalf.

You've lived an adventure that has left you breathless and exhilarated.

You've also probably been pushed to the breaking point, and you might have even been broken. You might be a little bit surprised that it's been so hard and that no one warned you about all the booby traps. Oh, you knew there was an enemy—we all do—but you didn't expect him to eat your lunch quite so often.

I hope I don't sound too pessimistic or depressing. I'm really not. I know that God ultimately wins and that if I remain faithful, I'll win with Him and will, hopefully, bless many, many lives in the process. I have no regrets about running headlong down the road less traveled. It's just that, as I've run, I've seen a lot of wonderful people lying wounded and bleeding along the side of the trail. Come to think of it, I've taken a turn there, as well.

At times, I've been so disappointed with God that I didn't know if I could go on. My first daughter died in my arms when she was three years old, and I wasn't sure if I would ever live again. When my wife and I said our good-byes to her through our tears, I felt my faith evaporate, and it's been a slow process rebuilding it.

I've experienced rejection and slander in church, and it threatened to leave me a bitter man.

I've become weary of church services that inspire me to "press in" and yet leave me with no real power to change.

Religion has left me parched and dry and wondering if it was really what God intended for me when He drew me into the other life.

After years of faithful service and more than my share of wounding in church, I've wondered, *Is this all there is?*

And this is just *my* story. What about the millions of Christians who are attempting to love God and obey His plan for their lives? What about you? Where has *your* Christian journey taken you? What pain and disappointment have *you* experienced? What tough questions will you stand in line in heaven to ask God? There are many unanswered questions out there.

But you already know all of this, don't you? Most of us who have embraced the Christian faith do. We discovered it early on. We encountered Jesus, and eternity flared to life within us. Dissatisfied with all other living, we embraced the truth that we were destined for something more and that God had a special assignment for us to fulfill on the earth. We even took steps to discovering and fulfilling that destiny. We embraced the road less traveled, and we determined—as Christopher Columbus did—to sail off the map. For some, that decision has been glorious. For others of us, it has caused us to be pierced, and the pain of the wounding has nearly shipwrecked us.

The funny thing about all of this, though, is that I still know there is more. I know that I've only barely begun to scratch the surface of the wonder and mystery and majesty of God, and I know that when I get into His presence everything will be okay. I know I haven't been lied to. I know that the Promised Land awaits me and that, just as there are giants ahead, there are also glorious victories to be won. I know that if I'm faithful to my calling, people will be healed and restored to God. I know that I haven't even begun to see what God is planning for me.

I'm sure you know this, too. It speaks to your character and your faith and the fact that your relationship with God is real. You're a hero. Do you believe that? Do you believe that you should stand alongside those people listed in Hebrews 11? I'm sure you remember that Scripture—the roster of the mighty men and women of faith. Do you remember what it says they did? Through faith these saints: conquered kingdoms . . . performed acts of righteousness . . . obtained the promises . . . shut the mouths of lions . . . quenched the power of fire . . . escaped the edge of the sword . . . out of weakness became strong . . . became powerful in battle . . . put foreign armies to flight. Quite a résumé, isn't it?

Unfortunately, there's more to the text. The Bible goes on to say that they were also: tortured . . . imprisoned . . . stoned . . . sawn in two . . . persecuted . . . left destitute and afflicted. But then the Bible gives them the ultimate commendation when it says that they were those "of whom the world was not worthy" (Hebrews 11:38).

Do you know that God views *you* that way? Do you know that He's mindful of the price you've had to pay and that heaven is probably sick and tired of hearing Him brag about you? He loves you! His call to the other life was not a trick—*there is more awaiting you!* It will be more exciting than anything you can imagine. Your life will impact the world in a way that you'll never understand until you see it from His eternal perspective in heaven.

A few weeks ago, I felt like the Lord spoke to me in one of my morning prayer times. I was journaling my thoughts to the Lord and then recording what I felt He was speaking to me in response. I was asking about a new direction my life and ministry had taken, and I was wondering if I was really on track: *Is this really of You?* His response pierced my heart as He said to me, *This is your road less traveled by.*

I love that poem by Robert Frost. Do you remember how it ends?

> Two roads diverged in a wood, and I,
> I took the road less traveled by,
> And that has made all the difference.

There's a longing in the heart of humanity that nearly drives each of us mad. There is a hunger for *life*—true life that goes beyond possessions and pensions and retirement.

It's the whisper of eternity that stirs restlessness in our souls. There's a thirst that has left us parched and dry. We were made for more than the way we're living.

Two roads have diverged in the woods of our lives. One path is the typical, pat answer of religion. The other is the wild, untamed road of relationship with the only One who can satisfy the thirst.

Let's not give up. I know that a thirst for eternity has been awakened in us, and sometimes our Christian experience doesn't help at all to satisfy it. Let's hold steady.

Jesus knows all about this thirst.

Questions for Consideration and Application

1. Have you heard the "other life" speaking to you?

2. What did it say?

3. Has your religious experience stifled or accentuated its voice?

4. Are you ready to take the road less traveled?

5

TROUBLED WATERS

Shadow owes its birth to light.

John Gay

There will be no song on our lips if there be no anguish in our hearts.

Karl Barth

I thirst."

Isn't that an amazing statement? "I thirst."

It doesn't seem like the kind of thing we would expect the Savior of the world to say during the very act of rescuing humanity. I mean, it's not very heroic. Did you ever hear of Batman, while in the midst of saving Gotham City, saying, "Hang on, boys, I really need a drink."

"I thirst." It's so vulnerable. So fragile. So . . . *human*.

I guess it shouldn't surprise me too much that Jesus voiced the cry of His thirst while on the cross. After all, He came to walk in the shoes of humanity and to bear our burdens, grief and weaknesses. He knew that mankind was dying of spiritual thirst—in fact, the primary thrust of His ministry had been to quench that thirst.

To the woman at the well, He offered living water that would forever satisfy her. On the last day of the Feast of Tabernacles, He cried out, completely disrupting the order of the service, "If anyone is thirsty, let him come to Me and drink" (John 7:37). To those of the self-satisfied religious movement, He came to awaken their deeper thirst, while to the desperate, longing masses, He came to slake their desire with the very touch of God.

"I thirst."

Don't you?

I think our thirst has ruined us.

Sometimes I wish I had never tasted His living water. I wish that I could be satisfied with my lesser desires, and I wish this longing for eternity hadn't erupted so violently in my soul. Now that I've tasted of Him, I am wrecked for other pleasures and other approaches to life. He's awakened eternity in me, and now I can't be satisfied by anything less.

I suppose this is a positive thing—it's probably what He was shooting for all along. I guess it's good that I'm hungry for life and thirsty for the Spirit of God. My problem, though, is that my *experience* of abundant life, as typically walked out in the life of my church, doesn't seem to match the level of hunger in my soul. I'm doing my best to fulfill everything my church has said I should do, and yet, frighteningly, it's not enough. I'm still thirsty. And if I didn't know where to go to find a drink, I might panic. Many people do.

All over the world, people wrestle with their spiritual thirst. Some take it to the local pub. Some take it to hedonism and thrill-seeking, while others take it to an endless string of dead-end relationships. I took mine to church—and it worked for a while.

A great feeling of personal satisfaction ensues when we are fulfilling the commands of God, and when we practice the principles of Christianity, we *will* experience positive results. Our relationships will improve if we implement what Jesus said about serving our fellow man. Our businesses will flourish if we practice what the Bible teaches about excellence and stewardship. Our families will be healthier if we follow the biblical principles that govern family dynamics. The principles really do work.

The problem with principles, though, is that they are only rules that help us navigate our lives—*they aren't life itself*. I love the principles of honor and love and communication that help to keep my marriage to Jessica strong and secure, but I can't curl up in bed at night with a principle—I need a passionate relationship with a living and breathing person.

I did a little math once. I'm still not sure what prompted me to do it, but I must have had too much free time on my hands. On a whim, I decided to calculate a rough estimate of how many church services I had attended throughout my lifetime. When I combined my weekly church attendance (I've been going to church since I was two years old) with all of the programs, Bible studies, men's meetings, camps and retreats, and added in the years I spent in Bible college, I guessed that I had participated in over five thousand church services. Five thousand church services! That's a lot of church.

I know it helped me. I can't imagine what my life would be like or what temptations I might have fallen into had I not been raised in a Christian home. Church has always been the backdrop of my earliest memories.

My parents were saved in the early 1970s, when the nation was reeling from the Vietnam War and the aftermath of the sexual and drug revolutions of the 1960s. My dad was a Vietnam veteran, and both of my parents came out of the hippie movement in search of something more than life had offered them.

One of my earliest memories was of my parents being water baptized in a swimming pool by a precious, elderly Baptist preacher named Millard Bedwell. He was a proper, distinguished gentleman who wore a three-piece suit even in the heat of summer. My long-haired, spiritually hungry parents would sit barefoot on his living-room floor as Mr. Bedwell would explain the Scriptures to them and tell them of God's love.

He baptized them when I was about two years old (I think I remember the baptism because it traumatized me—I thought my folks were being drowned in the water). The conversion that my parents experienced was so deeply profound that from that chlorine-soaked moment on, Christian spirituality became a core value of my upbringing.

My parents talked about God and modeled a pure, loving marriage. They carefully monitored what movies we viewed and what music we allowed into our home because they wanted us to please the Lord as a family. We were deeply committed to our local church, and when it launched a private school during my first-grade year, my parents were quick to sign me up.

My childhood was marked with memories of family camp, teen camp, vacation Bible school, participation in Royal Rangers, harvest parties, summer outreaches and lots and lots of church meetings. I was blessed with a rare and wonderful childhood. I could feel God's hand on my life from a very young age as I canoed and swam and ran along the riverbanks of my childhood. I was profoundly blessed by my family and the childhood I experienced—to be honest, I can hardly find a bad memory from the early years of my life. (The soul-crushing crucibles of life came a little later for me.)

Church was very significant for me. I was water baptized in the river in the middle of winter while there was snow on the ground. I preached my first sermon when I was fourteen years old, during a Wednesday-evening service dubbed "Teen Leadership Night." I remember when I thought God's *presence* had something to do with *presents*, and I can remember when I first began to actually discern His real presence. I've always loved the Church.

How strange then as I approached the crisis of adolescence (while attending a private Christian school) and a later crisis (after six years of Bible college) when my first daughter died in my arms at three years old. I discovered the frightening reality that, despite practically living my whole life in church, *my thirst had scarcely been quenched at all.* Perhaps, I wondered, I had been drinking from the wrong source.

In John 4:14, Jesus said to the woman at the well, "But whoever drinks of the water that I will give him shall never thirst; but the water that I will give him will become in him a well of water springing up to eternal life." The word that Jesus used for *well* is a word that refers to an artesian well that springs up from the depths of the earth into a rushing fountain. It's not a pool of water into which we dip our lives—it's a flowing current of life that overwhelms us.

Some of us have turned to our church in search of this fountain of life. Some have run headlong into the arms of Jesus, but others have been caught in troubled waters. Here's what some of us have found.

The Church Is a Vegetarian Buffet

Do you remember that cute old lady from the 1980s who issued the famous query, "Where's the beef?" Do you remember how she would look down derisively at an undersized, shriveled beef patty swallowed up by an enormous hamburger bun, and then stare into the camera to deliver her profound question?

It was a great question—and it worked. It got our attention. "Where's the Beef?" bumper stickers were everywhere as the people found their voice—no more wimpy hamburgers!

Where's the beef? Where's the substance? Am I really getting my money's worth? Is this all there is? These are pivotal questions—although perhaps they are a little dramatic when applied to a fast-food restaurant.

But what happens when these questions are superimposed upon the church? What happens when it's not a cute little grandma posing the question to a TV audience, but it's a hurting, searching son or daughter who desperately wants to find the meaning to life? What happens when people bring their thirst to our church and we offer them a good, solid *religious* service that leaves them echoing that sentiment from the 1980s?

It's happening every day, you know. People are leaving church by the thousands. They've tasted what church has to offer and, still dissatisfied, they are abandoning organized Christianity in droves. Some of them are new converts who expected church to sustain the incredible intensity of their conversion experience, while others have been in church for a long, long time and have finally concluded that they've had enough.

Some feel that they've been mistreated or misunderstood, while others are simply bored. Whether from hurt or disappointment, or just the simple fact that no matter how hard they look, they can't seem to find the beef, they quietly slip out the back door in search of something more.

Church historian George Barna has found this to be such a widespread occurrence today, with literally *millions* of believers following this course of action, that he has categorized this group as *the Leavers*. They're not searching for a different gospel or a different God—they just want more of Him. In his book *Revolution*, Barna calls them Revolutionaries and describes them this way:

> Many Revolutionaries have been active in good churches that have biblical preaching, people coming to Christ and being baptized, a full roster of interesting classes and programs, and a congregation packed with nice people. There is nothing overtly wrong with anything taking place at such churches. But Revolutionaries innately realize that it is just not enough to go with the flow. The experience provided through their church, although better than average, still seems flat. They are seeking a faith experience that is more robust and awe inspiring, a spiritual journey that prioritizes transformation at every turn, something worthy of the Creator whom their faith reflects. They are seeking the spark provided by a commitment to a true revolution in thinking, behavior, and experience, where settling for what is merely good and above average is defeat.[1]

Perhaps as you read Barna's statement, you realize that *you* are one of those Revolutionaries who is meant for a deeper experience. It may explain to you why you've felt such a discontentment in your religious experience. It may also have brought some peace to you to realize that you haven't been wrong in your frustration—there *is* more than what you've experienced. There has to be more!

Jesus didn't come to earth to institute a religion—He came to reveal God. And if our religion is all about learning to know this God more, then it should constantly become more exciting and dynamic, not less. If we are truly experiencing the Creator of the universe on a daily and weekly and monthly basis, then the fruit of our Christian service should be anything but dry and lifeless. We should be the picture of a spiritual oxymoron: fully satisfied and yet fully thirsting. We should be satisfied because we have touched our Creator, but desperate because we want more of Him.

I realize, of course, that the intensity and depth of our Christian experience shouldn't be contingent upon what our church does, and that, ideally, we should engage in the spiritual disciplines and walk of faith on our own initiative. However, God created us to be part of a community, and from the beginning He determined that it wasn't good for man to be alone. We need the Church!

When Adam faced the oversight of the Garden, God brought him Eve.

When Moses balked at his commission to overthrow Pharaoh, God sent Aaron with him.

David needed Jonathan.

Jesus called the twelve disciples, and when He sent His followers out on His behalf, He never sent them alone—at the very least, they had a ministry comrade as they journeyed two by two.

We need each other. We need the Body of Christ, and for many, the life believers receive in the corporate church experience is vital to their spiritual growth and maturity. How tragic then, that for some, that cute little old lady took the words right out of their mouths: "Where's the beef?"

The Church Isn't Living What It's Preaching

What's the deal? If the lives of some of the people I have met in church are examples of the victorious Christian life, I want out before I even begin! Sadly, this is the commentary of some people's experiences in church. It's been mine—how about yours?

Have you ever seen Christians who didn't live what they were preaching? Have you ever been rejected by Christians who preached unconditional love and acceptance? Have you ever listened to great sermons on moral purity and integrity and then watched your church elders flirt with pretty girls at the office? I've experienced some of this. I've watched church leaders who preached a consistent message for years and placed incredible pressure on their followers to comply with that message, and yet, when it came their turn to respond, they never followed the teaching of their own sermons. I walked in on one of my church elders once in a very intimate and flirtatious conversation with a woman who wasn't his wife. I've been shocked by the shady character of some supposed saints, and I've seen the damage it has caused in many lives. I've watched good, solid people become bitter and disillusioned by the lack of integrity in their spiritual leaders.

It's not just church *leaders* who need to practice what they preach. I've hired the services of Christian brothers and sisters, thinking that their work would bear the stamp of excellence and integrity, but instead I saw no discernable difference between their work and any other business in the yellow pages. I used to get excited when I saw the Christian fish symbol on certain advertisements until I realized that, very often, it doesn't mean anything. It doesn't necessarily mean that the work will be done with excellence and efficiency, or that the worker who displayed the fish will perform his or her work as if it is worship to the Lord.

We need to practice what we preach.

The Church Has No Relevance for My Life

I spoke with a friend the other day who made a disturbing, yet profound statement. He said, "Ninety percent of the glory of my life occurs within the walls of my home, on the streets of my neighborhood and within the confines of my business office, and yet only about 10 percent of what

I hear in the average Sunday-morning sermon applies to these parts of my life."

Our God is a God of encounter, and He expects His people to be changed forever every time they meet with Him. If we, as the Church, are providing messages and methods that fail to produce life and practical equipping in the hearts of people, we run the risk of escorting them outside the room in which we're so desperate to keep them. "The church has no relevance for my life." What a tragic statement! And what an untrue one. God has placed the keys to life in His Word and in the hearts of His people—it's just that in some places, the church isn't really being the Church.

The Church Has No Power to Change My Life

I don't just want to grow as a Christian; I want my life to change. I don't just want to know more about God; I want Him to be a reality in my everyday existence. I want to get out of debt. I want to prosper financially. I want to see people's lives improve as a result of their contact with mine. I want to heal from the wounds of my past. I want my children to be spared the pain I experienced as a result of my sin. I want to see miracles, signs and wonders in my lifetime. In other words, I want something *to happen*. I don't just want to talk about it all of the time.

And I don't want the people whom I invite to church to leave thinking the same thing.

The true Church, God's sons and daughters who have His Spirit living inside them and who are growing daily to resemble Him more, *do* have the answers for our society. The church, as it exists in some circles today, might not be enough to slake our thirst—but its God, whom it exists to worship and make famous, *is more than* enough.

6

Snakebites

We must love men ere they will seem to us worthy of our love.

William Shakespeare

Be not disturbed at being misunderstood; be disturbed rather at not being misunderstood.

Chinese Proverb

Study to be patient in bearing the defects of others and their infirmities be what they may: for thou hast many things which he must bear withal.

Thomas á Kempis

One of my favorite places in the world is the Garden of the Gods Park in my hometown of Colorado Springs. Its red rock formations are stunningly beautiful—like something out of Jurassic Park or some prehistoric age. It's one of those places where you can't help but be captured by the beauty and awe of God. It's gorgeous. It's awesome—a popular destination for hikers, cyclists and tourists.

It's also home to some rattlesnakes. Although I've never personally seen one there, I always keep my eyes open because every year I hear the report of at least one snakebite.

Have you ever hunted rattlesnakes? When I was in college, a friend taught me a simple way of hunting them. You carry a long, forked stick in one hand and a rifle in the other, so that when you find the snake, you can simultaneously pin it down and blow its head off.

The apostle Paul was bitten by a snake once. Do you remember the story? At the end of the book of Acts, the story is recorded of Paul's shipwreck. He was on his way to a court appearance before Caesar, and was shipwrecked and washed ashore on the island of Malta. It was cold and rainy when he and his shipmates rolled onto the beach with all of the flotsam and jetsam of their damaged supplies, so to stave off the bitter chill in the air, Paul built a fire and began gathering sticks to fuel it. Acts 28:3 says, "When Paul had gathered a bundle of sticks and laid them on the fire, a viper came out because of the heat and fastened itself on his hand." Another translation says that the viper was "driven out by the heat" (NIV).

Paul, in classic apostle style, shook the snake off into the fire and then began to lay his hands on some sick people and heal them. It's a fascinating, inspiring little story.

I just wish it always worked out like that in the real world.

I've never been in a natural shipwreck, but I have felt like my world has crashed down around me many times. And while I've gathered sticks to recapture the fire I've lost, I've been bitten—not on my hand, but in my heart. I've seen many spiritual vipers in my tenure as a Christian. You probably have, too. In fact, we could probably show each other our twin-fanged scars that we carry as evidence of our survival after snakebites. I would rather face a natural rattlesnake at the Garden of the Gods than the ones that have pierced my soul.

Some people have been bitten and been able to move on—successfully eliminating the dangerous venom from their bloodstream. Others have just now noticed that a writhing shape is dangling from their wrist. Others are swelling up as we speak. Still others have only begun to carry a bundle of sticks—they are completely unaware that they are clutching something poisonous to their chest.

Wherever you may be in this classification—whether safe and recovered, bitten and in danger, or completely unaware that you're playing with fire—the Lord wants you to know several things:

1. Snakebites are common to humanity.

The first snakebite in Scripture occurred in the Garden of Eden, when our original parents were pierced by the serpent's accusations against God and the venom of offense began flowing in their veins. The serpent said, in essence, "God is holding out on you. There's something wonderful in the Garden—but He'll never share it with you." Sadly, they bought the whole story. The first offense in Scripture was man's offense against God, and unfortunately for you and me, we now carry a vulnerability to offense, as well. We're also still prey for snapping snakes. God even said so Himself.

Even though God came to man's defense, cursed the serpent and said that the serpent's head would indeed be crushed one day, He also said that, at times, the serpent would get ahold of our heels (see Genesis 3:15). Although we're promised victory, we're also promised a few snakebites along the way.

Snakebites are common to humanity. Jesus said, "Offences come" (Matthew 18:7, KJV). Offenses *do* come! The tragic thing is that they often come through the people with whom we are the closest. We never feel truly offended unless we're hurt by someone we love. We're not really betrayed unless it's by someone whom we've allowed past our guard.

There's a frightening Scripture to be found in 1 Peter 2. In it, Peter quoted the Lord, saying, "I lay in Zion a choice stone . . . a stone of stumbling and a rock of offense" (verses 6, 8). That doesn't sound right, does it? *God* lays a rock of offense in the middle of His Church? Shouldn't the Church be the last place that we should face offense?

I struggled with this verse for a long time until I caught a glimpse of what it might actually mean. Perhaps God allows a rock of offense in His Church because He knows that *if we can deal with the venom, we can kill the snake!* The poison doesn't have to take us out!

2. Snakebites can be fatal—and must be healed immediately.

Although snakebites are common to humanity, I don't want to crush the snake's head and then die from its poison in the aftermath. That often happens, you know. We can win a victory and survive an attack, but then be taken out by the aftereffects of offense.

I'm convinced that the number-one cause of spiritual death among Christians is not outright demonic attacks, but snakebites. The devil can't just waltz in and shut down God's work in our lives. He can't stop the will of God or take the anointing from us—but he *can* bite our heels and inject us with his poison. We humans have an Achilles' heel that is vulnerable to the venom of vipers.

Do you know anyone who was bitten and then walked away from the faith? Have you been tempted to do just that? The book of Acts says that the islanders expected Paul to "suddenly fall down dead" (28:6). People usually don't fall down *suddenly* unless the venom has been working in them for a while.

When Christians commit adultery, it isn't usually because a demon of lust just suddenly decides to take them out. More often, they just get bitten—and offense enters through a hurt that is never cleansed and healed. Then, on an especially low day when they are vulnerable to temptation, their resistance is down, and they surrender to the moment.

It's possible that this is what happened to King David when he sinned with Bathsheba. It's possible that some unhealed wounding had weakened his resistance during that particular springtime when the kings were supposed to go out to war. I can't prove it, but it seems likely that David had some unresolved wounds in his heart. Perhaps they started when he was young and continued through his adulthood. We know that he was overlooked by his dad when Samuel came to anoint the next king: It wasn't until Samuel insisted there might be another son that someone finally ran and pulled David off the back forty. His boss and mentor spent years trying to assassinate him. His wife Michal despised his passion for the Lord, and one of his loyal subjects cursed him and threw rocks at him during his lowest moment.

I can't prove that David was offended by all of these (and many other) shots of venom he had taken, but at the end of his life, in a Godfather-esque moment on his deathbed, he did order some pretty vicious paybacks (see 1 Kings 2:1–9). Perhaps a twinge of offense had crept into David's heart through his wounds of rejection and colored his judgment on that night when Bathsheba was bathing. Perhaps he had become tired of always paying the price for holiness and felt that he *deserved* to act out in an impure way.

Whether or not this was true of David, I do know that offenses *will come*—and if we don't resolve them immediately, they can kill us.

Sometimes we get bitten on the heel—when we're moving and making progress in the Lord. Sometimes, like Paul, we get bitten on the hand. The "hand" in Scripture is a picture of our authority, strength and power. The enemy's goal is to weaken our authority and derail our progress so that he can ultimately poison our purpose.

Paul unwittingly clutched the viper to his chest—we cannot fulfill our destiny if we do the same.

3. Snakebites hurt.

This point is "painfully" obvious, but please bear with me. Before the venom can enter our bloodstream, the snake's fangs must pierce our skin. Snakebites are extremely painful, and because the hurt is very real, we run the risk of overlooking the fact that any offense we pick up because of the pain becomes sin. Just because we've been genuinely hurt doesn't mean we have the right to hold on to offense or bitterness—it's poison in our veins, and as long as it flows through our bloodstream, it will prevent us from being healed.

4. Hurt paves the way for offense.

Being hurt is not the same thing as being offended, but if we aren't careful, our unhealed wounds will eventually grow the fruit of bitterness and offense.

5. Vipers usually strike right before a moment of spiritual breakthrough and advancement.

God knew that if Paul could survive the snakebite, the chief's father would be healed and an entire island would be invaded with the power of the Gospel.

6. Servants get bit a lot.

The viper was hiding among the sticks—if Paul hadn't been serving by gathering sticks, he wouldn't have been bitten. It's usually when we're serving and giving and sacrificing that we are most susceptible to the sting of the snakes. The interesting thing, though, is that while servanthood makes us vulnerable to being bitten, *it also protects us from the poison.*

7. The heart of a servant, with its accompanying grace and humility, acts as an antidote to the venom of vipers.

Servants remember that Jesus faced the ultimate snakebite while laying His life down for mankind—this memory, and their commitment to partake in His sufferings with Him, enables them to persevere through the pain.

8. Vipers are revealed when things get hot.

The fire drove Paul's viper to the surface. Don't be condemned if, as you go through the fires and trials of life, you suddenly realize that you've been clutching a snake to your chest. Sometimes you can't discern the viper until the heat's turned up, but when it does, it's unmistakable. The little creature opens its mouth wide—and looks for some flesh to latch on to.

9. We must forbid gossip in the Church.

The taste of revealed flesh drives vipers out into the open. Let's create an atmosphere where the nakedness of our brothers and sisters does not become a water-cooler conversation piece. Let's practice the love that covers a multitude of sins and see if we can't minimize the target for our enemy.

10. Sometimes we can simply recognize that we've been bitten and cast our offense in the fire, but at other times we need help to get free.

Paul was able to shake the snake off of his hand and into the fire. Whether we need a good shaking or intensive surgery, let's commit to getting rid of the venom as quickly as possible. Let's ask the Lord for thick skin and soft hearts.

11. Snakebites are not necessarily indicators that we've done something wrong.

In fact, we are often bitten when, like the apostle Paul, we are doing something right.

12. The snakebites that hurt us don't come from snakes.

Satan's snakebites usually come from other people. You and I will probably go our entire lives and never receive an actual snakebite from a viper in the wild, but you can bet that the enemy *will* sneak into our midst and use a person to pierce us. When this happens, let's remember this final point:

13. God has promised us victory over snakebites.

Jesus said that those who believe in Him will "pick up serpents, and . . . [they] will not hurt them" (Mark 16:18).

Early in our marriage, Jessica and I wrote a poem that declared our war on the venom of vipers:

> When all is said and done in this season of strife,
> And cemeteries tremble at the presence of life,
> When light bursts our darkness and our sight is
> restored,
> We'll be found faithful, with our gaze on the Lord.
> When the Spirit checks our wounding for a sign of
> bitterness,
> And our loyalty is tested by signs of Judas' kiss,
> When done is what He promised and our baby is
> healed,
> Then foxes, torched and running, will be seen in
> Satan's field.
> And all throughout our ages, with our future clear or
> dim,
> In hope and worship, though He slays us, we will
> trust in Him.

Questions for Consideration and Application

1. Can you identify any snakebites in your past?

2. Can you identify any in your present?

3. If so, what are you doing to expel their venom?

4. Do you believe that you can finish your life in victory with your wonder of God still intact? God does!

Let's still be here fifteen years from now! Psalm 84:4 says, "How blessed are those who dwell in Your house! They are ever praising You." Let's live out this verse! When someone tries to find us twenty years from now, let's have someone say, "Have you checked the sanctuary? You'll probably find them in there. After all of these years, they're venom-free, and they're still praising Him!"

7

TATTOOED:
A TALE OF TWO PIERCINGS

Sweet are the uses of adversity;
Which, like the toad, ugly and venomous,
Wears yet a precious jewel in his hand.

William Shakespeare

The nearest way to glory is to strive to be what you
wish to be thought to be.

Socrates

What you are, so is your world.

James Allen

Have you noticed lately how many people have tattoos?

Sorry. Dumb question. Of course you've noticed. It seems like everyone has one these days. It's not just burly ex-convicts sporting the word *mother* on their upper arms or loyal legionnaires with the name of their platoon emblazoned on their forearms anymore. Tattoos have become an art form in our society, and you can see them almost anywhere skin is revealed.

My dad has one. So does my sister. They're everywhere. From NBA players to stay-at-home moms to clean-cut business executives, sporting tattoos has become a cultural norm.

There is another form of tattooing in effect, though, that we can't see with the naked eye. Oh, we can certainly see it—we can discern it—but it's more of an *internal* tattoo. It's a tattoo of the soul. We get these tattoos in the same way that people get them on their epidermis. We are cut—an incision is made into either our skin or our soul—and ink is poured into the wound. When the wound heals and the scab falls off, the ink reveals a picture—a flower, or a skull and crossbones, or the state of our soul. I have several of these internal tattoos, and they reveal more about the state of my heart than I'd like to think. You probably have them, too.

Job had several of these tattoos. He wrote about it in chapter 19 of his book when he said, "Oh that my words were written! Oh that they were inscribed in a book! That with an iron stylus and lead they were engraved in the rock forever!" (verses 23–24). He went on to say, "I know that my Redeemer lives, and at the last He will take His stand on the earth. Even after my skin is destroyed, yet from my flesh I shall see God" (verses 25–26). Job understood that what was cut into his flesh would last for a long time, so he wanted to make sure that the message of that cut was this: My Redeemer lives! He said, in essence, "I've been cut so badly that my skin has been destroyed, and yet from my flesh—the very place of the cutting—I know that I shall see God. Let the message that gets poured into my flesh be one of faith and confidence in a good God. Let it be recorded forever in the tablet of my flesh that God will come through for me."

What a man Job was!

What about you and me? I know that we have been cut—I certainly have, and I know you wouldn't have hung in here with me for so long in this book unless you, too, had experienced the piercing cut of betrayal, disappointment, loss or rejection. We've all been cut—that's a given. The question is, what will we do with it? We have to be extremely careful with what gets poured into the wounded places of our hearts, because whatever lands there will be very difficult to get out. Some tattoos are nearly impossible to remove.

If we could see with spiritual eyes into the tattooed state of each other's souls, we could read the picture that our cutting has painted there. The pictures that our soul tattoos reveal answer this question: *Am I broken, or am I wounded?*

This is such an important question because Christlike *brokenness* can be used by God to powerfully catapult us along the path of our destinies, while *woundedness* will derail us before we ever begin. There is no brokenness without wounding; however, it is possible to be wounded and never truly become broken.

A Tale of Two Piercings

Imagine two men. Both love God, and both have pure hearts before Him. Both desire to fulfill their destinies and make their lives count for eternity. They are good men, faithful men. They love their wives, and they father their children well. They work hard, and they are fiercely loyal to their friends. You would want to have each of them on your team. They're a lot like you and me. But both of them have been pierced, and the pain has run equally deep in them.

One of them has worked such a process of submission to the Lord in the midst of his pain that his cut has turned to brokenness. He reeks of the presence of God. He cries often, but there is such a tenderness and contrition in his heart that those around him say, "Surely he has encountered the Lord." He isn't perfect, but he is broken—and he is on the verge of promotion.

The other man is wounded. He still loves God, but he hasn't embraced the crushing of Gethsemane yet. He has forgotten that even Jesus had to have His very life squeezed out of Him prior to His ascension to the ultimate seat of authority in the universe. He is a good man, but he is in danger—his wound might steal his destiny. Try as he might, there is no way around his pain—his only choice is to embrace it and allow it to transform him, or to decide that this is the point in the journey where he quits. By the way, pain *always* transforms us—either into broken vessels that God can use or into wounded warriors who have been disqualified by our response to *someone else's sin*.

As we eavesdrop on some contrasting responses between the broken man and the wounded man, let's keep three central facts in mind:

1. *Every* piercing will produce either brokenness or woundedness.
2. Wounded people *can* become broken people. In fact, it is God's passion to help them do so.
3. Broken people need to guard their brokenness so that they don't slip back into the cycles of woundedness.

Let's observe the difference between brokenness and woundedness in the face of the following situations:

When Confrontation Is Needed

A broken man embraces correction because he is keenly aware of the rough spots in his life and he desperately wants to spare those around him the pain he himself has experienced.

A *wounded man* fears correction because of the pain in his heart—he just can't handle any more of the refiner's fire.

A *broken man* seeks out correction so that he can become more like Christ.

A *wounded man* shuns correction because he feels he has already paid enough of a price.

A *broken man* corrects others with extreme gentleness, patience and grace.

A *wounded man* can be harsh and inflexible because his pain does not allow him to risk the extension of grace.

A *broken man* surrenders his rights for the greater good.

A *wounded man* fights for his rights because justice has never been served.

When Relating with Others

A *broken man* is a lover of people and is willing, as the apostle Paul was, to impart "not only the gospel of God but also [his] own [life]" (1 Thessalonians 2:8).

A *wounded man* relates to others from a protective posture that allows people in only so far. Often his fear of being hurt again goes so deep that this self-protective device operates on a subconscious level.

A *broken man* constantly expresses gratitude and appreciation because he is so grateful for the grace of God in his own life.

A *wounded man* has difficulty saying "thank you" because it is a form of vulnerability.

A *broken man* isn't afraid of his blind spots and his bald spots. He realizes that everyone else can see them anyway.

A *wounded man* is desperately afraid of exposure, and therefore he guards and postures defensively.

When Judging Others

A broken man never judges others, but immediately prays when he hears of the shortcomings of someone else. He has received the mercy of God in his own life, and he now desires to share the same with others.

A wounded man is still looking for a sense of personal restitution and, consequently, is quick to pass judgment on those around him.

When Facing the Memory of the Offender

A broken man is able to face the pain of the offense with perspective and humility, realizing that if it weren't for the grace of God, *he himself* might be someone else's offender.

A wounded man faces the pain of the offense with a longing for vindication—he doesn't want revenge in an unhealthy sense; he just wants recognition that he has been wronged. This is a natural desire, but a dangerous one, because this recognition often never comes. If we continue to hold out for the offending party to ask our forgiveness, we might wait in a wounded state for a very long time.

When Speaking about the Offensive Situation

A broken man never talks about the offense unless it's at a time when his pain can minister to someone else and help that person make the transition from wounded to broken.

A wounded man talks about the offense all of the time. He may not necessarily speak of it in an impure way—he just can't stop talking about it. He has never received closure, and he is desperately looking for it.

When Spiritual Leaders Are the Offenders

A broken man realizes that spiritual leaders are only human, and he does his best to extend grace.

A wounded man can't get over the fact that "they should have known better because they are leaders."

A broken man will talk about the situation only with people who either are part of the solution or can help him process what happened in a safe, wholesome way.

A wounded man attracts other wounded people, and inappropriate comments frequently follow them.

A broken man commits to working through the healing process and giving his heart away again.

A wounded man writes his leaders off and makes judgments about all spiritual leaders because of the situation.

A broken man uses the pain to become a better leader himself.

A wounded man thinks only in terms of self-preservation.

A broken man goes to his leader and risks the pain of either reconciliation or rejection.

A wounded man holds on to the poison for fear of being hurt again.

A broken man is courageous enough to forgive.

A wounded man lends a supportive ear to others who have also been hurt by their leaders.

A broken man leaves silently and sweetly when it becomes apparent that he needs to part ways with his church leaders.

A wounded man leaves a trail of burned bridges behind him when he leaves.

When Others Are around Them

A broken man is the sweetest individual to be with—he exudes grace, love, acceptance and the refreshing peace of God.

A wounded man will wound other people. He doesn't mean to, but he will—his unhealed wound leaves him guarded, edgy and protective. It's not that he doesn't love other people, but he just needs to experience the love of God for himself in a fresh way.

I realize that this list is far from an exhaustive treatment of the subject, and I know that I am surely oversimplifying many things and overlooking many others. My goal has simply been to paint a brief picture that might help us to judge the state of our own hearts.

If you read through my list and realized that God has worked a grace of brokenness in your life, I am proud of you! That's awesome! Now you must be careful to remain in that humble posture as you await the promotion that always follows true brokenness. If, however, you became a little overwhelmed because you realized that you still have a long way to go in your quest for brokenness, I want you to know that it's okay. I have areas where I'm just beginning, too.

Let's commit together that we won't let this point in our journey be the place where we quit.

Let's commit to the fact that it's too soon to declare failure and that we won't begin to shut off our hearts for fear of being wounded again.

Let's commit to embracing Christlikeness—the image of God in us—as we choose to forgive and grow from the situations that have scarred us.

Let's determine that *our responses to someone else's sin will not take us out.* The world is in need of life, and it doesn't need guarded, wounded people who can't relate to others' pain.

The world needs broken vessels that have stayed positioned in the Master Potter's hand and can now be used to pour out pure, untainted life into the parched places of the hearts of other people. It needs people who have drunk deeply from the cup of misunderstanding and are more beautiful from the experience. In the next chapter, we will further discuss this beautification process.

Questions for Consideration and Application

1. What do your soul tattoos reveal?

2. In what areas are you wounded?

3. In what areas are you broken?

4. Are you committed to moving from woundedness to brokenness so that the beauty of the Lord can shine through you?

8

It's Hard to Be Beautiful

The perfection of outward loveliness is the soul shining through its crystalline covering.

Jane Porter

What is beautiful is good and who is good will soon also be beautiful.

Sappho

I don't think I've ever known a woman who thought she was a natural beauty. There are certainly natural beauties out there—I'm fortunate enough to live with one—but I don't know of any woman *who thinks she is a natural beauty.* There is something in the psyche of women that makes them think that they need lengthy times of preparation to truly look their best. Please don't tell her I said this, but my wife looks just as stunning when she rolls out of bed in the morning as she does in her makeup, jewelry and high heels. I think the women in our lives need to know that they are gorgeous whether they're in a T-shirt and sweats or in a red-carpet evening gown. Having said this, though, I think it's possible that there is something of God's design in a woman that makes her *want to prepare to look her best.*

Even Esther, who replaced the beautiful Queen Vashti, had to undergo a lengthy season of preparation before she was ready to appear before the king. A review of her story tells us that she, along with all of the other most beautiful virgins of the realm, underwent two separate six-month seasons of beautification before she was presented to the king. Despite her natural beauty, it took time and focused effort for her to see the full potential of her beauty released.

Likewise, it takes time and focused effort for us to move from a wounded state to a broken one, in which the beauty of the Lord shines through us. The Lord spoke to me about this once through John 15:3, in which Jesus said, "You are already clean because of the word which I have spoken to you." The word *clean* in this passage is the Greek word *katharos*, and it is a synonym to a word that means "to be cleansed by shaking to and fro as in a sieve or by winnowing." As I meditated on those words, I felt the Lord speak to my heart: *I have allowed the shaking in your life to dislodge the judgment and criticism in you. There's been a lot of you in you, and I've had a lot of shaking to do to get you ready for what I want to do in you. You've experienced what you have experienced because of what I've called you to.* This exhortation from the Holy Spirit reminded me of one of my favorite word studies in the Bible.

It comes from Romans 2:4, in which Paul spoke of the "kindness of God" that leads us to repentance. The word *kindness* here is the Greek word *chrestotes*, and it has a fabulous meaning. The word, descriptive of Jesus Himself and the standard to which we as His followers should strive to attain, refers to aged wine that, over the course of time, has lost all of its bitterness. It speaks of grace that pervades our entire nature until we have lost our harsh edge. It is the opposite of severity or the tendency to quickly cut people off. I love that! There is nothing harsh or austere in Jesus—and there should be nothing like that in you or me, either. We should grow more beautiful as we age.

Let's take a look at a few pointers that will help us embrace the beautification process of the Lord. One thing that we will notice is that it is often the pain we have experienced that brings the beauty of brokenness to the surface in our lives.

Please forgive the simplicity of the following observations—I merely want to lay a brief foundation that will provide a few practical ways of moving us out of woundedness and into the brokenness through which *He* can shine.

First, we have all been wounded.

From the first time they flicked your foot to make you cry just after you were born, to the piercings of old age, pain follows the footsteps of humanity. God promised that, while we would ultimately experience victory over the serpent, it would occasionally latch on to our heels (see Genesis 3:15). I'm not sure how you interpret that verse, but it doesn't sound pleasant to me. In His famous lecture on prayer, Jesus included a portion on forgiveness—our need to forgive those who hurt us. Why did He include this? Because we have all been wounded.

Second, wounds hurt.

Why do I state such an obvious observation? Because many professing believers in Jesus live in a tragic state of denial when it comes to the wounding of their souls. On multiple occasions, the Bible tells us that the Lord "restores my soul" (see Psalm 23:3; Lamentations 1:16). The word *restore* is the powerful Hebrew word *shuwb,* and it carries the image of floodwaters receding back to the point of departure. It literally refers to a dam that has cracked and broken and, consequently, lost control of the flow of the tide. When the Bible tells us that God restores our souls, it means that God heals the broken places in our hearts, the places where the life of God has leaked away. We wouldn't need restoration unless we had been depleted. We wouldn't need healing unless we had been hurt. Wounds hurt—in fact, they can hurt so badly that some people carry the sting of divorce, bereavement, betrayal and rejection for a lifetime without ever experiencing lasting freedom.

Third, the more we love the offender, the deeper the hurt is that we experience.

I care what people say about me. I know I shouldn't, but I do. If someone I've never met, from a church I've never been to, has heard a rumor about me, it bothers me. I want everyone to like me and think I'm a really great guy. What really hurts me, though, is when people whom I know and love and trust are upset with me. What devastates me is when people to whom I've given my heart and exposed the state of my soul turn on me. Thankfully, it doesn't happen very often—probably because I couldn't handle it if it did—but when it does, it can take me a long time to heal. Is that true of you, too? I'm sure it is. It's not profound; it's just human nature. Had a Pharisee kissed Jesus in the Garden of Gethsemane, it would have stung, but it wouldn't have held a candle to Judas' treacherous smooch. The more we love the offender, the deeper he or she can hurt us.

Fourth, some wounds will go away over time, but others require outside assistance to be healed.

This is an important observation and one worth considering because it's important to know which wounds will just go away and which ones require surgery to mend. I love to work out, and I often experience muscle soreness when I have worked hard, fatigued my muscles and had a quality workout. There are other times, however, when the pain is deeper than soreness, and I can tell that I have injured a joint or a ligament. At those times, I realize that I may need some help to recover. I might need to see a chiropractor or, at the very least, lay off the weights for a while.

There are misunderstandings and hurts that occur on an almost daily basis that we process and release—we choose to let go of them and move on from them. With God's help and the exercise of our own will, we are able to successfully navigate the minefield of these lesser wounds. But there are other wounds that can take us out if we don't receive help. These wounds usually fall into one of the following categories:

1. The wound came from someone you knew and trusted.
2. The wound came when you were extremely vulnerable in your trust—such as when you were a young person, or a young believer, being mentored by an older believer.
3. The content of the wound questioned your integrity and character.
4. While processing the wound, you knew you were right but were unable to get a fair hearing—the offending party wouldn't take any ownership of his or her part.
5. There was no closure for the wound, so you were forced to process it all on your own.
6. The wound came from spiritual leaders who abused their position of power.

The wounds that are inflicted by our spiritual leaders are especially difficult to heal because there are very few safe places to talk about them. We all remember what happened to Miriam when she spoke out against Moses—she became snow white via leprosy (see Numbers 12:10). We recall that the Preacher in Ecclesiastes told us not to curse the king, even in our bedchambers, lest a little bird of the air hear and carry the matter to him (see Ecclesiastes 10:20). Then we have the awesome example of how David refused to touch the Lord's anointed (see 1 Samuel 26), so we're left feeling like we've been unjustly wronged, but we are uncertain about how to go about righting the wrong. It seems we are left with only one of two options: stuff the hurt and try to go on as a dutiful soldier, or talk about it and risk being labeled an "Absalom," David's son who betrayed him and stole the hearts of the people of Israel. What should we do?

I will attempt to answer this question as it specifically relates to church leaders in another chapter, but here I want to simply say that *we must fall on the Rock and allow the Lord to put us back together.* David said to Gad, "I am in great distress. Let us now fall into the hand of the LORD for His mercies are great" (2 Samuel 24:14). How do we fall on the Rock and allow the Lord to put us back together after we've been hurt?

1. We must repent.

Although we are the ones who have been hurt, we must ask the Holy Spirit to convict and cleanse us from our own sin. We can't get our hearts right toward our offending brothers and sisters unless we are keenly aware of our own shortcomings.

2. We must choose to forgive.

This one is tricky because we *can't* forgive on our own—we need the grace of God to help us do it. However, we still must set our hearts and minds to it.

3. We must remember that we forgive in layers.

Wounds often occur in layers. Therefore we need to forgive as often as the sting of the wound arises. I've been shocked and discouraged at times when old wounds that I thought I had long settled and released have resurfaced. I think to myself, *Have I really made such little progress?* But that's a wrong way of thinking, because we forgive in layers, and what was forgiven at the skin-and-tissue level must also be forgiven at the bone-and-marrow level. The resurfacing of an old wound may not be an indicator of a *lack* of progress on your part, but of increased maturity—perhaps the Lord thinks you're ready to handle a deeper level of healing and cleansing.

4. We must process the hurt with someone who can help us.

You need to be able to talk to someone who can help, but you must make sure it is someone who can help you process the situation from a mature perspective. What exactly is a mature perspective? It's one that will comfort you while simultaneously helping you see the big picture of what God is doing in your life. Yes, your heart may be bleeding all over your lap, but what is God doing *in* you and what is He requiring *of* you in the situation?

I recently received a word of the Lord from a trusted friend who usually brings great encouragement to the table when we talk. This time, though, his word was different. He said, "Hey, I was praying for you, and the Lord told me He was going to have you drink a cup of misunderstanding." At the time, I was irritated, and I assumed he hadn't heard from God. Interestingly, though, within a matter of days, a situation arose in which I was completely misunderstood. (I honestly was—I know we always judge ourselves by our own motives, but in this situation, I really *was* misunderstood and wrongly judged.) There was nothing for me to do but drink the cup.

The man who gave me the word was a trusted friend in whom I could confide without fearing that I was gossiping or being inappropriate. He helped me see God's perspective in the situation, and he helped me see which attitudes I needed to adjust. Because there is almost always a kernel of truth in any accusation, he helped me see where I could change and grow. And then he encouraged me and loved me unconditionally through the situation. We all need someone like him in our lives—someone who can provide us with a safe place to be real.

The Preacher in Ecclesiastes lamented over the man who had no brother (see 4:8). For this man, he said, there is no end to his toil. We need a brother, and we need to feel free to allow him to help us navigate the murky waters of interpersonal grievances and offenses. We're not supposed to do this thing called life alone.

I should add one word of caution at this point and mention that the Holy Spirit is the Friend who sticks closer than any brother, and we must *always* defer to His leading in our lives. There have been many times when I wanted to bare my soul to a friend and I felt the Holy Spirit rein me in. I realized in hindsight that my would-be confidante was in a vulnerable place himself and wouldn't have had the grace to help me process the situation without becoming offended himself on my behalf. There have been other times when I realized that my own heart wasn't pure, and had the Holy Spirit not convicted me in time, I would have spewed poison onto anyone who would listen.

We need to be very careful *how* we process our hurts and offenses, but we don't need to be *afraid* to process them. Jesus will help us! He has promised that He will not leave us. He told His disciples (including you and me): "I will not leave you as orphans; I will come to you" (John 14:18).

Jesus came to me once when I was about to go down for the count. It happened at a conference when the speaker started his speech.

"I've seen enough in church to make me an infidel," the man said, "but I still have a made-up mind and the determination to see what lies at the end of a successful Christian race!"

His name is Dr. Seville Phillips, and I think he's made that statement every time I've ever heard him speak. He's an awesome man—he's been preaching the Gospel for nearly sixty years and he is more in love with Jesus than ever. He and his beautiful wife oversee a Bible translation ministry and numerous orphanages, and they preach the Gospel all over the world. He's been mentoring me from afar for over ten years now (although he doesn't know that), and every time I've ever heard him speak, I have come away strengthened, refreshed, inspired, challenged and assured of the fact that *I can successfully run my Christian race without losing the wonder.*

He preached one of his unforgettable messages once when my wife and I were going through an extremely dark time in our lives. Our first daughter, Alexis, was nearly three years old, and we had no idea that we had only six more months left to live with her on this side of eternity. She was extremely ill, and the draining fight of faith that we had waged for her since the first day of her birth had taken its toll on us. In addition to Alexis's condition, we were also facing some misunderstandings and rejection within our church. Although we still trusted in the goodness and sovereignty of God, we were tired. No, we were exhausted, and when we entered the auditorium to hear Dr. Phillips preach, we were at a breaking point. We resembled nothing like overcoming people of faith—we were just trying to survive.

When Dr. Phillips announced the theme of his message, my wife and I both buried our heads in our hands and wept—the grief and frustration pouring out of us freely. His sermon title was "The Crisis of Spiritual Fatigue," and it was one of the greatest communications I have ever heard. It was so timely and appropriate for our situation that, very possibly, God may have told him to preach it just to save us from being shipwrecked in our faith. I hope Dr. Phillips can mentor me in person in heaven someday. Oh, I know the angels will be there, along with all of the saints from antiquity, but I'd still like to have him as a mentor. I'll always be grateful to him because he helped me retain the wonder of my faith, especially during such a difficult time. He reminds me of D. L. Moody, who, when asked how he continued to preach and teach and minister even in his old age, responded, "I never lost the wonder!"

When we run headlong into the maze of church politics, the betrayal of family members in our church, the weariness of constant spiritual battles and the general wounding that occurs simply from being human and living with other humans in our churches, one of the first things to go in our spiritual lives is the awe and wonder of simply knowing Jesus and being who He's called us to be.

Second Peter 1:21 tells us that "no prophecy was ever made by an act of human will, but men moved by the Holy Spirit spoke from God." The phrase *moved by the Holy Spirit* literally means "to hoist an empty sail" so it can catch the wind of the Spirit again. The men of God who penned the pages of Scripture raised the sail of their lives so that the breath of God could fill them and direct them where He wanted them to go. Let's do the same thing in the following pages. Let's rehoist the mainsail of our life and ask the Holy Spirit to fill us again with a fresh awe and delight for the presence of God. Let's recapture the wonder of knowing Jesus! When we do so, it will fill us with the grace and perspective necessary to engage in true worship— the healing of broken relationships.

Questions for Consideration and Application

1. Have you asked the Lord to search *your* heart regarding your hurtful situations?

2. Is your hurt something you can process on your own, or do you need outside assistance to help you get through it?

3. Do you have someone who provides a safe place for you to process your questions?

4. Are you relying on the Holy Spirit as your closest Friend to lead you through your pain?

5. Are you beginning to reflect the Lord through your increasing Christlike brokenness?

9

HEALING BROKEN RELATIONSHIPS: THE ESSENCE OF TRUE WORSHIP

Grant us grace, Almighty Father, so to pray as to deserve to be heard.

Jane Austen

[Jesus said,] "Therefore if you are presenting your offering at the altar, and there remember that your brother has something against you, leave your offering there before the altar and go; first be reconciled to your brother, and then come and present your offering."

Matthew 5:23–24

Do you realize that Jesus prioritized conflict resolution between the members of His family *above* the corporate worship experience? He emphatically stated that if we have *anything* that is out of order with a brother (on our part or his), we are to stop all of the trappings of religion and pursue the healing and restoration of that relationship. He said that we should leave our gifts at the altar and seek out our brothers or sisters to resolve the conflict.

This was a pretty powerful concept that He introduced, since worship is the core foundational stone of our Christian faith. We're worshipers first and foremost. *Before* we are evangelists who set out to save the world, we are worshipers. *Before* we are mighty warriors bearing the standard of the King, we are humble, worshiping servants. *Before* we are prophets and teachers and leaders, we are those who live to worship and adore our Savior. Jesus said that the Father was *seeking* true worshipers (see John 4:23). The apostle Paul could hardly complete a chapter in his letters without erupting into praise and adoration of the Lord. We are worshipers to our core, and the Father is looking for people like us.

Some people don't realize this. They think that they're just a sports fan or that they really enjoy working hard or that they appreciate a few hobbies. They don't realize that in all these things, *they're worshiping*—we all are. We were created to worship.

When God made mankind (both male and female) in His image, He made them to be like the moon that absorbs and reflects back the glory of the sun. This is part of the literal meaning of the word *image*. It references an object (like the moon) that has no glory of its own, and yet it shines with glory because of its uplifted gaze (its worship) of a greater glory. We're moons. We're gazing in adoring wonder at our Creator, and He is filling our lives with purpose, strength and grace. At least hopefully that's what's happening. Hopefully we're gazing at *Him*.

Because worship was a foundation stone on which man was created, because God is seeking worshipers and because worship, engaged in with all of the angels and saints of history, is a part of our eternal destiny in heaven, it's shockingly profound that Jesus prioritized the healing of offenses *above* our involvement in corporate worship.

Even though we were made to worship Him, Jesus doesn't want our worship if it's laced with unresolved relational conflict. He believes that the first act of worship must be a settling of our past-due accounts with the brethren.

The Gospel message is one of relationship. It's a desperate cry from the heart of a passionate Father to be reconciled with His wayward children. It's the call of heaven to hell-bound humanity: "Return to Me!" Jesus was torn and shattered so we could respond to this Father's cry.

No wonder He ranks restoration right up there with corporate worship.

When you and I leave our gift at the altar and do our best to restore broken relationships, we are engaging in the essence of the Gospel, and we are tuning in to the very heartbeat of God. Reconciliation, whether in the form of an unsaved person finding Christ or two Christian brothers burying the hatchet, is the essence of true ministry.

The phrase *be reconciled* is profound in that it means to mend a breach from a quarrel where the fault may be either one-sided or two-sided. Sometimes the fault is one-sided. And sometimes there are honest miscommunications and hurts that occur through no true fault of the offending person. I was recently an ignorant, one-sided offender.

I received a letter from a woman who needed to express some hurt and anger that she had felt toward me. Her letter was very gracious and kind, but it expressed how hurt she had been by some counsel that I had given her. Earlier that year, she had confessed to me her struggle with a particular sin, and in an attempt to minister grace and compassion, I told her that it "wasn't a big deal." I thought I was being merciful, but understandably, she felt that I was making light of her struggle.

I was so grateful for her letter! Although it stung a little (as it always does to be confronted), I embraced the opportunity to make things right with her. I was thrilled that she left her gift at the altar and sought me out to resolve the hurt—even though, on my part, I was ignorant of the hurt she had experienced.

She could have held on to it. She could have left our church in silence, or, on her way out the door, she could have told a dozen people that I was a crackpot counselor. Thankfully, she chose to worship—in the truest sense of the word.

I realize that this example is fairly tame, and I'm not trying to imply that church issues are usually that simple or easily resolved. I know that they're not. My point is simply that sometimes the offense is one-sided and sometimes both parties are wrong.

In another of my leadership misfires, I failed to follow up on some things that I had promised to do for someone in our church. It was a significant situation, and this person was counting on me to come through; however, I either became too busy or I forgot or I just plain procrastinated, and this person was legitimately hurt. I felt terrible, and I knew I had blown it, but before I was able to mend the situation, I discovered that a dozen people had already been brought into the loop and that I, and consequently the leadership of the entire church, had been slandered.

I'm not trying to pin the fault on the other party—*I* was the one who initially blew it—but when ten people heard of my failure before I had been given the chance to make it right, we were suddenly in a quarrel with plenty of error *on both sides*. Our relationship was at a crossroads, and only mutual repentance and forgiveness would help us navigate it.

Fortunately, we did. Fortunately there was enough grace for each of us to own our share of the wrong (me for failing in my commitment, and this person for talking to other people instead of me) and to forgive (me for being gossiped about, and this person for being disappointed and let down in a vulnerable time).

I wish I could tell you that all of my relational conflicts in church have been resolved this easily and completely. I wish I could stand before Jesus someday and tell Him that I *never* hurt any of His sons and daughters, but unfortunately I'll have to ask Him to forgive me, and I'll have to hope that He covered and healed those whom I wounded through my sin and shortcomings.

It might be a very terrifying moment for me and other church leaders to give our account to Him. I might have to tell Him why I ignored the Matthew 18 principle. Do you remember that one? Do you remember that Jesus laid out a very clear-cut means of conflict resolution that applies to *all Christian brothers*? The Matthew 18 principle is not for *all Christians except pastors or church leaders*. It's for all of us, and we've got to get back to this principle and begin modeling loving reconciliation. Here's what it says: "If your brother sins, go and show him his fault in private; if he listens to you, you have won your brother. But if he does not listen to you, take one or two more with you, so that by the mouth of two or three witnesses every fact may be confirmed" (verses 15–16). If we can't do this among ourselves and be reconciled in our personal relationships, how will we ever have credibility with the world when we attempt to fill our role as ambassadors crying out, "Be reconciled to God"?

For many, this principle from Matthew 18 has been discarded, and it's especially painful when it's discarded by church leaders whom we look up to with trust and respect.

Questions for Consideration
and Application

1. Are there any areas of misplaced worship in your life?

2. Are there any broken relationships that need to take precedence over your involvement in corporate worship services?

3. Are you willing to worship—in the truest sense of the word—and heal these relationships? If so, you'll invite the pleasure of heaven.

10

YOUR PASTOR

He that hath no brother hath weak legs.

Persian Proverb

He who serves his brother best,
Gets nearer God than all the rest.

Alexander Pope

Peace hath her victories, no less renowned than war.

John Milton

Remember those who led you, who spoke the word of
God to you; and considering the result of their conduct,
imitate their faith.

Hebrews 13:7

He wouldn't return my phone calls."

"I've emailed and left messages but I haven't received a response."

"They didn't want to talk about it."

"They said there's really no point in meeting to discuss it."

"I guess it's best if we just move on."

I've heard all of these phrases and more in conjunction with hurting church members who failed in their attempts to discuss their grievances with their church's leadership. Why does it often seem to be so difficult for church leaders and their people to host a meeting of the hearts and minds in which they can facilitate, at best, a reconciliation or, at worst, a peaceful, hurt-free parting of the ways?

I think it breaks God's heart, and it probably ticks Him off, as well.

This could be a dicey topic because, very often, the majority of deep church wounds do not occur from interpersonal relationships among general members of the congregation. They occur with the leadership of the church. Although we all realize that pastors are people, too, and that they are just as much in process as we are in our spiritual growth and development, somehow their failures still wound us deeply, and we still hold them to a higher standard in our hearts.

That's okay, you know, because God does, too.

James urged us to be careful before we presume to teach anyone, because teachers are held to a stricter judgment. Paul was very clear in his communication to Timothy and Titus not to install anyone into positions of church leadership unless his character and devotion were up to the task (see 1 Timothy 3; Titus 1). Moses made one small yet memorable mistake, and he lost the privilege of entering the Promised Land (see Deuteronomy 4:21–22).

Or was it really a small mistake?

Do you remember the story? The people were thirsty, and God wanted to satisfy them, so He told Moses to speak to the rock. Instead, Moses struck it. It wasn't quite what God had said to do, but it still worked. Water flowed from the rock, and the people's thirst was quenched. But what happened next is a little surprising: God got so hacked off over Moses' action that He forbade him from entering the very

Promised Land, the pursuit of which he had given the last forty years of his life. Why did God respond so dramatically? I think it's because there was something else that happened when Moses hit the rock and the people slaked their thirst in its geyser—they thought God was mad at them.

The image of a ticked-off Moses swinging his miraculous staff with all of his might and crashing it into the side of the rock sent an indelible message to them that, yes, God would give them water, but He wasn't very happy about it. Moses hurt the people's view of God that day. He misrepresented God to the people, and he paid dearly for it—he saw his promise only from a distance and was never allowed to enter into it.

God holds His leaders to a higher standard of judgment *because He loves His people so much*. He is like a jealous father who scrutinizes every movement of his child's new teacher before he is comfortable leaving the child in his or her care.

God wasn't mad at the Israelites at that moment. Oh, He had certainly been angry before, but this time He didn't want to discipline them; He wanted to talk to them. "*Speak* to the rock, Moses. Show them that I am a God of relationship and that I want My words to bring them life." Instead, Moses spanked them, and for some, they may have been nervous to ever bring their thirst to God again.

In the film adaptation of C. S. Lewis's *The Lion, the Witch and the Wardrobe*, the fox says to Mr. Beaver of his recent encounter with Aslan: "He's everything we hoped he would be." Unfortunately, the opposite of this sentiment is sometimes true in church. Thirsty, hurting sons and daughters bring their desire to church in the hope that it's okay to be dry and thirsty and desperate, only to find a picture of God that is *unlike* anything they hoped He would be.

Very often, we, the church leaders, are to blame for this.

Now let me say again that this is certainly not always the case—the Church of Jesus Christ is filled with amazing leaders who love Him with all of their hearts and who are doing their absolute best to represent Him well and to unconditionally love every person who graces the doors of their congregation. And lest anyone think I am pointing a finger, let me quickly point it at myself first. *I* have misrepresented God to His people at times. I've been Moses having a bad day, and I'm sure I've hurt some people in the process. Even the most Christlike leaders are still humans with sin natures and bad-hair days and attitude problems that can hurt the people around them. It is incumbent upon spiritual leaders, though, to remedy every hurt as quickly as possible and to always lead from the perspective of a student. Yes, I'm a leader, but I'm a follower, too. Yes, I am a shepherd, but I am following the Good Shepherd, Jesus Christ, just like you are.

What do good spiritual leaders look like? Spiritual leaders are very important for our spiritual growth and maturity so it's important for us to know what to look for in one. I'm very selective and protective about the people I let speak into my wife and daughters' lives. What does the ultimate pastor look like? How can I identify him? Let me try to describe him.

First of all, *he loves you.* I mean genuinely. You feel it every time you're around him—he's crazy about you, and it always makes his day when you walk into the room. It happened just last week when you showed up for the service. His whole countenance brightened, and the smile on his lips said it all—church could begin now that *you* had arrived. He made a point of seeking you out and hugging you with a purity and affection that melted your defenses and filled you with a sigh of relief. You knew that you were loved. You knew that you mattered.

This feeling of being loved and noticed is so healing because you spend the majority of your life in settings where you constantly pour yourself out and sacrifice yourself, and you wonder if anyone notices. He does. And he thanks you for it. "I want you to know I see the sacrifice you are making, and I am so grateful for it" are not uncommon words for him. You've heard him say this to you, and you've heard him say it to countless others. He *does* see and appreciate and honor and respect the heavy load that his people carry on a weekly and daily basis, and he doesn't just cheer you on from the bleachers—he's out on the field running beside you.

He's transparent. Who can relate to an untouchable spiritual giant who never struggles with anything less than trying to find more ways to change the world? I can't. I need someone who knows how I feel, who loses his temper once in a while, who has been known to make a bad decision and then have to humble himself to make it right. I need to see someone who isn't always full of faith and on top of his game. This pastor I'm talking about is very touchable. He's probably so touchable because he is a real person with real issues and real emotions and passions, but he also possesses a real trust in God and a real desire to know Him more each day.

He's very approachable. He's approachable because he's so *nonjudgmental*. When you speak to him about your weaknesses, he never patronizes you or belittles you—he cries with you. He prays for you as passionately as if your issue were his own. When he sees people bound in an obvious sin or shortcoming, he doesn't smirk or shake his head; he begs God to have mercy on them because he knows that he himself could be in their shoes were it not for the grace of God.

He's not mad at people who are trapped in gay lifestyles—he weeps over them, and he relates to them with great tenderness and care because he knows that they must be experiencing many conflicting emotions in their hearts. He doesn't get disgusted with the young girls who strive to emulate the seduction of the silver screen—he views them as daughters in need of a father. He never judges *you*. You feel unconditionally accepted by him, and this sense of security makes it easier for you to trust. It makes it easier for you to heal from the blows you've taken in life. *Healing flows from him*, and the more you're around him, the more you want to provide that same healing and unconditional love to the people in *your* world.

He sees the greatness in you. Every time you're around him, you feel your chest swelling with a sense of confidence, and a can-do attitude seems to envelop you. He really believes that you will change the world. He doesn't put you in any boxes—he loves the real you and celebrates your uniqueness. I should probably also say, though, that he is never content to let you remain the same. He wants you to grow. He believes there is greatness in you, and although he is the epitome of gentleness, he is committed to seeing you reach that greatness. It's what David referred to in Psalm 18:35: "Your gentleness makes me great."

He has a dream-releasing ability that makes you believe that the impossible is within the realm of possibility. You really can have the abundant life, leave your mark on the world and enjoy the Lord and all of His benefits. He thinks you could fly if you put your mind to it!

He thinks you're beautiful. This characteristic may seem weird, but it's true. He thinks you're gorgeous. And you need that! With all of the pressure that our culture places on outward beauty and the exterior signs of success, you need someone to see you for who you really are and to think you hung the moon. Your pastor does. He thinks you're awesome.

Because you are!

As a leader, he is not controlling. Nothing about him wants to stifle the creativity and freedom that you have in Christ. He views his role as that of a coach who is successful only when his athletes are setting personal bests and breaking world records. He wants to break world records *together with you.* It's not just about him; it's about his team—and he is thrilled that you are a part of it. He is committed to you, and he is there when you need him.

When he speaks, it is as if God Himself was speaking to you. His are not the rehearsed words of a dime-a-dozen Sunday-morning sermon. He brings fresh bread from heaven every time he stands behind the pulpit. On the one hand, you love it because it provides you with strength, courage and the practical tools you need to overcome in life and be a better person, but on the other hand, it's a little un-nerving because you wonder, *How did he know that? Who's been talking to him about me? Has he wiretapped my phones, and has he been listening in on my conversations?* When he speaks, he does it, as Peter said, as "one who is speaking the utterances of God" (1 Peter 4:11).

When he walks in the room, the love of a father walks in with him, and you can breathe easy. You are safe. You are loved. You are protected, and you are in the presence of someone who thinks you're a hero.

Who wouldn't bring their life under the submission of such a leader? I would! In fact, I already have. You must realize, I'm sure, that no one human can adequately do all of the things I have referenced. Oh, we may do some of them fairly well—we may even do one or two of them exceptionally well—but *there is no human leader who can fully provide all that we need as growing disciples of Jesus.* We need our true Pastor. We need the Good Shepherd. We need *Him.*

We need the One who holds the universe and our hearts with equal care.

We need the One who has measured the depths of the oceans and the depths of our greatest fears.

We need the One who has counted the number of stars in the sky, the grains of sand on the seashore and the hairs on our heads.

We need the One who limited the power of the surging waves and who can limit our every opposition.

We need the One who can pastor nations and still remember our birthdays.

We need the One who not only declared His love for us, but who backed up His declaration with His own blood.

We need the only One whom we can truly call "good."

Does this mean we don't need His helpers—His under-shepherds? Of course not! What I just listed for you when I described the ideal pastor is a compilation of the top qualities of *each* of the pastors I've had in my life. I've served great men and women of God who revealed Jesus to me. Through their combined efforts in my life, I have discovered my destiny, I've become infatuated with God, I've grown as a disciple, I've built a lasting foundation of truth in my life and I've been spared the pain of spiritual shipwreck—on numerous occasions. The more we grow in God and the more committed we are to His plan for our lives, the more we need spiritual leaders to keep pointing the way to His likeness and nature. We need our pastors. We need their wisdom, their covering and the words that the Lord gives them. We need to respect them, honor them and recognize them as agents of the Lord's guidance and protection in our lives. We need to be careful, however, that we don't ask them to be God for us. They're not, and they can't be. Every time we ask them to be, we thrust the knife of disappointment into our own hearts.

Myles Munroe says, "Wherever purpose is not known, abuse is inevitable." The purpose of a pastor is not to try to be God for his or her followers. When that happens, spiritual abuse will soon follow. The role of a pastor is to help lead us into an ever-growing resemblance of the *true* Pastor.

If we have been hurt by church leaders, let's remember three things:

1. *They are human, too.* This does *not* let them off the hook or marginalize the wounds they may have caused us, but it may help us to take our focus off of them and place it more securely on our Good Shepherd.
2. *Even the worst leaders can be tools of destiny in our lives.* Just ask David. I would wager that when it was all said and done, he wouldn't have traded one day that he spent with Saul. He allowed the weakness of his leader to fashion true leadership in his own heart.
3. *Some day we ourselves may be in leadership positions.* When that day comes, let's enter it with a track record of grace, forgiveness and perspective following us.

In my book *Second in Command: Strengthening Leaders Who Serve Leaders* (coauthored with Dutch Sheets and published by Destiny Image), I outlined several steps to help us move toward reconciliation with our spiritual leaders. Some of these steps apply specifically to our interactions with our spiritual leaders; all of them contain wisdom to help us navigate relational conflict.

When counseling a hurting brother, ask:

1. Have you gone to the person involved to try to resolve the conflict?
2. Do you know all of the facts?
3. Do you know what the other party was thinking?
4. Have you spoken with anyone else about this?
5. What does the Bible say you should do in this situation?

Finally, before you offer them any counsel, remember that Proverbs 18:17 says, "The first to plead his case seems right."[1]

When addressing an issue with an offending brother or sister, adhere to these principles:

1. *Remember that the relationship is more important than the issue.* As much as it is possible, let the issue take a backseat to the relationship. Of course, if it is an issue of conscience or morality, it must be resolved satisfactorily, but if it is an issue of style, preference or opinion, it should never take precedence over the relationship.

2. *Use nonoffensive terminology.* Any time you can avoid phrases that elicit defensive responses, you will be ahead of the game. Phrases like, "You always do this" or "You make me feel like . . ." will get you nowhere. No one *always* does a particular action. Few people *intentionally* set out to make someone else feel bad. If you need to address issues of personal conflict, say something like, "I was a little confused when you said this or did that." This gives them the opportunity to share their heart and motives without feeling attacked. When they clarify their intentions, you can then say, "Thank you for clarifying things for me. Without knowing your heart, I was beginning to feel hurt or frustrated" (or whatever the emotion might have been).

3. *Allow them to respond in turn.* We all have blind spots. If we're identifying a blind spot in someone else, there is probably a high likelihood that we have one, too. Sometimes I've been shocked because I have pressed for discussion and an opportunity to express to someone how I had been feeling, only to discover that *they* had been feeling hurt by *me*. When confronted, humility says, "Thank you. Tell me more."

4. *Establish a peaceful course of action.* In a setting of trust, love and mutual respect, it is easy to walk out the commitments that lead to health and relationship.[2]

When addressing an issue with an offending church leader (or leaders), follow these pointers:

1. *Appeal—don't confront.* The Lord didn't assign you to your leader to change him; however, there *will* be times when decisions or attitudes need to be challenged. If you need to confront, do it with a humble, appealing manner, as a son entreating a father.
2. *Appeal in private.* I heard someone say that "loyalty in public yields leverage in private." If you need to challenge them, do so, but do it in private.
3. *Don't accuse or attack.* Couch your appeal in the form of a question. Ask them to explain why they did or said the things they did. Tell them, "I was a little confused when you said that, because it came across like . . ." A blunt rebuke doesn't go very far with anyone, including your spiritual leaders.
4. *Use the term* we *versus* you. Instead of saying, "I think you handled that poorly in there" or "I totally disagree with you on this one," use phrases like, "I was a little concerned by our last meeting" or "Let's process a little because I'm not sure things were handled quite right."
5. *If they hold fast to their decisions, support them (unless their decisions are unbiblical or unethical).* There are some decisions with which you will disagree from a practical, logistical standpoint. Those you can flex on. There are other decisions, however, that cross moral lines. Don't let your name be associated with those.
6. *If they defer to your suggestion, share the credit with them.* Don't share with anyone that you disagreed with them

and that they came around to your way of thinking. Walk in humility and honor them.

7. *If they are unwilling to address the issue and you feel you have no choice but to leave, leave appropriately.*[3] Let me comment on this delicate point by quoting from Gene Edwards's *A Tale of Three Kings*. In this classic story on biblical authority, Edwards aptly writes about the only appropriate way to leave a kingdom after all biblical options for restoration and resolve have been tried to no avail:

> How does a person know when it is finally time to leave the Lord's anointed . . . ?
>
> David never made that decision. The Lord's anointed made it for him. The king's own decree settled the matter. . . .
>
> Only then did David leave. No, he fled. Even then, he never spoke a word or lifted a hand against Saul. And please note this: David did not split the kingdom when he made his departure. He did not take part of the population with him. He left alone.
>
> Alone. All alone. King Saul II never does that. He always takes those who "insist on coming along."
>
> Yes, people do insist on going with you, don't they?
>
> They are willing to help you found the Kingdom of King Saul II.
>
> Such men *never* dare leave alone.
>
> But David left alone. You see, the Lord's true anointed can leave alone. There's only one way to leave a kingdom:
>
> *Alone.*
>
> All alone.[4]

Let's forgive our leaders even as we ask the Lord to heal us from the hurt they have caused. Let's release them from their shortcomings even as we vow to never duplicate in

Questions for Consideration and Application

1. Is your heart pure toward your spiritual leaders?

2. Have you placed any unrealistic expectations on them?

3. Are you looking for them to provide something that can come only from Jesus?

4. In holding them to a higher standard, have you moved into judgment and criticism?

5. Do you need to meet with any of them to heal a damaged relationship?

others the pain that they have caused. Let's be sure that our hearts are pure and that we are not flirting with Absalom spirits that have no qualms about backbiting and slandering spiritual leaders. God deals harshly with spiritual leaders who misrepresent Him to their people, but He also has little patience with wounded followers who unbiblically attack them. Let's be neither. Let's be humble followers who allow the shortcomings of our brothers and sisters in Christ (including our spiritual leaders) to fashion true Christlikeness in us, and let's be humble leaders who appeal, "Follow me as I follow Christ."

11

THE CUP OF MISUNDERSTANDING

A cup is in the hand of the LORD.
Psalm 75:8

"Are you able to drink the cup . . . ?"
Mark 10:38

"Remove this cup from Me. . . ."
Luke 22:42

I'm sure you've discovered by now in your Christian journey that every once in a while, you will pass a bend in the road and see an unmanned table in your way. Sitting on the table will be a nondescript chalice filled with a perfectly measured mixture. You will know its contents when you see it. You'll know this based on the scenery and the season surrounding that specific point of your journey.

Sometimes it will be a cup of promotion. Sometimes the cup will hold disappointment and correction. Sometimes it will contain unexpected refreshing and life, while at other times it will be a cup of sorrow and suffering. There's an especially bad mixture that is occasionally presented to us that might possibly exceed all of the others for its bitter scent, bitter taste and the bitter pain it leaves in your gut. *It's the cup of misunderstanding.* You might have heard of it. If you've ever tasted it, you know it's hard to forget.

This cup is different from some of the others because it's a very bitter cup and those who drink it must do so alone. Even with close friends around us, we still have to choke it down on our own. When Jesus faced His cup in the Garden of Gethsemane, His best friends fell asleep on Him—three times! He walked alone in the Garden and appealed to His Father to remove the cup from Him. He cried so hard that the capillaries burst around His eyes and He literally wept blood. To even get down a few swallows from this cup, the Bible says, the angels had to come down from heaven to strengthen Him. And He was God! No wonder this particular cup can be so difficult for us mere mortals.

Personally, I hate this cup. I've drunk deeply from a lot of nasty cups—demotion, rebuke, bereavement, betrayal, unanswered prayer and loss—but I think the cup of misunderstanding is the worst.

It tastes like injustice, and it leaves the most sinking feeling in your stomach. After a few sips, I don't know what to do with myself—I want to cuss or cry or both. It's a painful cup, it's a helpless cup, and I've discovered that this particular cup is usually passed out to *innocent* people. When I've done something wrong and then have to drink a punishing brew of humility, I can handle it because I realize that I'm simply reaping the consequences of my own foolish actions. When I've done well, however, and have *genuinely* performed in a Christlike manner, and I am *still* misunderstood and rejected, it hurts so bad I can hardly bear it.

Have you ever tasted this cup? Have you ever been blindsided by its aftertaste? It has one of those slow-release features in which the full bite of it isn't felt immediately. Oh, don't get me wrong, it hurts from the first sip—but usually you can muster some initial courage and choose to embrace the misunderstanding the same way Jesus did. It's what happens over the next few days that gets you. It sits in your stomach, and no matter what you do or how you try to pray or distract your mind, it haunts you. You feel so mistreated—because you are. It feels so unfair—because it is. You feel so helpless—because there really isn't much you can do.

Except drink it.

The cup of misunderstanding is especially harsh if it's delivered to you by a brother or sister in Christ . . . or by a friend or loved one . . . or by a spiritual leader. I've had all of these delivery boys come to my doorstep.

Paul said in Romans 12:18, "If possible, so far as it depends on you, be at peace with all men." Paul realized that sometimes it's not possible for us to be at peace with everyone. While God, of course, can do anything, and in time, every fractured relationship may be healed, there are present moments when we can't obtain the reconciliation that we desperately desire. Sometimes our attempts at restoration are met with further rejection, and all we are left with is an intimidating cup of misunderstanding.

I had to drink from this cup recently, and it devastated me. I had been misunderstood, misjudged and rejected all in one fell swoop. It came from someone whom I loved very dearly, and I felt as if I'd had the wind kicked out of me. The problem I found with this cup was that any attempts to sweeten the bitter taste with self-justification or defensiveness only backfired and caused further heartburn. Trying to explain myself only looked like defensiveness. Saying nothing looked like an admission of wrongdoing. Confronting the problem didn't help because the other party felt so sure of their position. There really wasn't anything for me to do but drink it.

And choose to love.

Someone once said that the pain of misunderstanding and betrayal hurts us the most because it's the most like what Jesus faced before the crucifixion. I could probably buy into that line of thinking.

Don't get me wrong—I'm not trying to sound like Jesus, who said so courageously while on the cross, "Father, forgive them; for they do not know what they are doing" (Luke 23:34)—although I'm sure that's the place He wants me to get to. No, I did my fair share of whining and choking and coughing and retching before I finished my first swallow. And my second, and my third . . .

But enough about me—what about you? Have you ever tried to resolve a conflict only to find that the other party had no intention of reconciling?

Have you ever tried to lovingly speak the truth into a delicate situation—thinking that those involved would appreciate your gentle honesty—but had it backfire on you?

Have you ever tried to live out the Scripture that says, "Blessed are the peacemakers," only to be crucified by *both* quarreling parties?

Have you ever tried to *biblically* restore peace after a conflict with church leaders, only to get the impression that they are above the rules?

Have you ever thought you were genuinely loving and serving someone, only to find out that he or she felt none of those things from you?

Have you ever been dazed and confused when doing a good deed cost you dearly?

Have you ever tried to step out in faith and bold obedience and been shot down or labeled as "arrogant" or "presumptuous"?

Has your character ever been unjustly called into question?

Have your motives ever been put on trial without being given any benefit of the doubt?

If any of these or other similar scenarios apply to you, then congratulations, you have probably received a nice mixture of a very bitter brew from the cup of misunderstanding.

In all fairness, I should acknowledge that sometimes *we* are deceived or presumptuous or naïve, and sometimes we're not as sweet and innocent as we think we are. Even at those times, however, this cup is brutal.

So, how do we drink it?

King David taught us how to drink from the cup of rebuke when Nathan confronted him over his sin with Bathsheba. He drank the cup of punishment like a true man and worshiped the Lord with every swallow. When he sinned again by numbering the people of Israel, he was given another cup of correction. This one cost him the lives of his citizens, and he drank it like a true king. He said, "I am in great distress. Let us now fall into the hand of the LORD for His mercies are great, but do not let me fall into the hand of man" (2 Samuel 24:14).

Peter taught us how to drink from the cup of failure when he denied Jesus and then raced full-speed to the empty tomb to try to find Him. He even failed when he tried to go back to fishing *after* the resurrection, but then he threw himself into the water and kicked and fought his way to the shore to be with the Lord.

Rebuke and correction and failure are all tough cups, but how do we drink *the cup of misunderstanding?* Once we're presented with it, it usually won't pass from us. We usually can't win this battle. All we can do is drink from its cup. Probably only Jesus really mastered this one. But here's how He did it.

He dealt only with His Father.

He recognized that He couldn't get through it alone—He needed the angels to strengthen Him.

He cried as much as He needed to.

He prayed until He could see through His tears.

He let His will die in the Garden.

He embraced His destiny.

He arose in so much strength that when His accusers came to accost Him, they were thrown backward onto the ground by the force of the power of God in Him.

Let's follow His lead. Let's cling to our Father. Let's recognize that sometimes we *can't* get through it alone—we need the angels to strengthen us. Let's pray as many times as we need to. Let's weep blood if necessary. Let's surrender our will and let *His* will come alive in us.

Someone once said, "You must embrace the cross if you would carry it with dignity." The same is true of this cup. No holding your nose. No gagging and spitting it out. Just drink it like a man (or a woman). Just ask the Lord to reveal to you any area in which you might be wrong. If He shows you something, repent and ask for the courage and power to change. Ask Him to send the angels, because you probably can't keep a pure heart all on your own. Ask Him to hold you tight if your friends fall asleep. Give Him your will. Cry as often as you need to, but when it's all said and done, make sure that His will lives in your heart.

Then arise in His strength.

Before we move on, there's one more thing I should mention. After you've drunk this cup successfully and the aftertaste is gone—you will look more like *Him!*

1. Have you ever faced a cup of misunderstanding?

2. Are you facing one right now?

3. Have you taken the necessary time to wrestle and pray and cry your heart out to the Lord?

4. Do you have a friend who can stand with you in your struggle? Even though you must drink the cup of misunderstanding alone, it's still nice to have someone else there.

5. Are you passing the test? As you do, you'll begin to look more like Him.

12

DEATH BY RELIGION

Ah, great it is to believe the dream,
As we stand in youth by the stream;
But a greater thing is to fight life through,
And say at the end, "The dream is true!"

Edwin Markham

Be good; get good and do good. Do all the good you can,
to all the people you can, in all the ways you can, as
often as ever you can, as long as you can.

Charles Spurgeon

We have committed the Golden Rule to memory; now
let us commit it to life.

Edwin Markham

I just finished watching an infomercial for Chuck Norris's Total Gym (his all-in-one piece of in-home exercise equipment). Have you ever seen it? It's a very compelling and inspiring little program in which Chuck Norris and Christie Brinkley spend about thirty minutes working out on the Total Gym. They challenge skeptical bodybuilders and professional athletes to try their fitness routine. Chuck performs biceps curls, triceps extensions and pectoral flyes and then flexes his rippling muscles while the apprehensive audience looks on. Time after time, the unbelieving weight-lifters and athletes participate in the Total Gym challenge and are put to shame by the intensity of its workout. They begin by saying that there's no possible way that the Total Gym could be as good as their free-weight routines, and they conclude by saying that Chuck was right all along—the Total Gym really works.

Chuck and Christie promise that by eating a healthy diet and exercising on the Total Gym for just twenty minutes three or four times a week, you and I can look great in spandex, too. Well, that's not exactly what they say, but the point is the same: Buy their product, use it faithfully and enjoy the results of feeling and looking fabulous. I actually own a Total Gym, and they're right—it does work. I'm still a little frightened by spandex, but my workouts on the Total Gym are great. By setting it up just right and completing the exercises properly, I, too, get a great pump, and I feel strong, healthy and inspired about my physical-fitness goals.

Please forgive this sacrilegious comment, but I've noticed that in some ways, the Church is a lot like that infomercial—we're touting a product that really works. It's not some type of gimmick or hype—it's the real deal. Jesus Christ *is* the answer for the woes of humanity. A life devoted to His service *is* the only way to ensure our eternal salvation and to experience the life we were created to live. We're not lying to the world—we *do* have the answers—and if people buy in to our product, they, too, can know and experience the God for whom they are searching. They genuinely need what we're selling.

The only problem with our infomercial is that we don't look like Chuck Norris or Christie Brinkley. We look more like a flabby, middle-aged guy who *thinks* he still looks good in spandex. People look at us and say, "If *that's* the fruit of their product, I think I'd rather have a Total Gym." We have the product, but we don't have the body to back it up.

We're promoting a better life, but ours isn't much better than theirs.

We're promising salvation, but we're delivering a list of rules instead.

We're claiming tight abs and spiritual victory, but most people can't see past our love handles.

We're selling *relationship*, but what they see is *religion* . . . and religion is killing our sales pitch. It's also hurting many, many people. It's important for us to identify what religion is (and isn't) because many of us have been strangled by it, and some of us may be unwittingly hurting others by our own religious airs.

Religion breeds death because it is limited to man's ability to comply with its codes and regulations. It works only to the degree that its participants strive to comply, so consequently, the only power available in religion is the power of man's discipline and determination. If people are exceptionally strong of will and are able to comply with the rules, their religion works. If they are bound in sin, however, and are in need of a stronger power to set them free, their religion condemns them and sentences them to "try harder."

Don't get me wrong—I desperately want to go all-out in my pursuit of God, and I want to consistently give an A+ effort in my fight against sin and temptation, but I'm also keenly aware that my best efforts still fall short of the cross. No matter how hard I try, I will always need a Savior who can rescue me not only from my sin, but also from my feeble attempts at fulfilling the requirements of my religion. Because religion of all kinds (including Christianity) is limited to man's ability to comply with its terms, religion of all kinds (including Christianity) separates us from the life of God and limits us to what we can do and become on our own.

It doesn't have to be this way. When our religion is a vehicle that leads us into true relationship with our heavenly Father, it is wonderful. It's when it becomes an end unto itself that it produces death. Jesus called the most religious people of His day "whitewashed tombs" (Matthew 23:27) because they were bereft of life. Religion breeds death because it is limited to man's ability to comply with its codes and regulations, and it works only for the strong, independent soul that is good at *doing*.

It's very easy for us to fall into the trap of religion because it's easier to manage a religion than it is to live in a relationship. Religion is easier to control than a relationship is—especially when that relationship is with the living God who wants to have a say in every detail of our lives. I think we all want God, but sometimes we want Him on our own terms—and religion allows us to do that. It keeps Him at a safe arm's-length distance while we busy ourselves in religious activity. Religion is okay for the committed *doers*, and it's also good for fearful leaders who can lean on the crutch of religious systems instead of the risky reality of life with a wild, passionate, all-powerful God.

So, how do we discern the difference between relationship and religion? After all, they can appear very similar on the surface, and I'm sure that even the best of us sometimes dangle a toe or two on the wrong side of the fence. I think that's okay with God, though. I think He loves it when all of our religious duty is done out of sheer love and passion for Him, but I think He's also okay when we read our Bibles simply because *it's the right thing to do*. I'm passionately in love with my wife, Jessica, and sometimes I love to do practical acts of service as small tokens of my devotion to her. There are other days, though, that I do my share of housework only because I know that I'm *supposed* to serve her.

It's okay to be in seasons when our Christian service is mere duty and when we're fulfilling the requirements of our religion only out of determined obedience. If we stay in that place too long, though, we run the risk of unwittingly slipping into a religious, death-producing system that will eventually cause us to make judgments about the person of God. Religion cannot adequately reveal God, and if we stay entrenched in it for too long without coming up for air, we will eventually lose the wonder of who He really is.

So, how do we know if a church or a group of believers is entwined with a religious spirit? First of all, I think we need to be very careful of labeling people. Let me share a very simplistic example. If you don't drink wine but I like to enjoy a glass occasionally, I can call you religious without knowing your heart. Perhaps you forgo wine because you deeply love Jesus and, for His sake, you never want to risk causing anyone to stumble. Out of your passion for Him, you have chosen to lay your right to the occasional glass of wine on the altar as an offering of love. Perhaps you don't drink wine because every time you want a glass, you are reminded that He is worth far more than any pleasure this world can produce. What's religious about that?

Perhaps I see you reading your Bible every day and I question your devotion as being religious because, after all, we're under grace and God doesn't get ticked if we skip a day of devotions. Of course, He doesn't get mad if we miss a day of reading, but what if you're passionately in love with Him and you can't wait to get out of bed every morning in the hope that His Word will come alive to you? What's religious about that? We need to be careful with what we label religious.

I do think it's safe to say, though, from the perspective of Jesus' conversations with the Pharisees (we won't take the

110

time to discuss those dialogues here), that religious systems and spirits are those that

1. place a man's vision above God's;
2. put heavy burdens on people instead of liberating them to run after Jesus;
3. sacrifice relationship for rules;
4. are heavy on control;
5. view people with suspicion instead of seeing their potential in God;
6. substitute principles for the vibrant reality of knowing God and for preplanned works for obedience; and
7. operate like a spiritual frat house.

This last point is very subtle, but because it has been a source of great pain to many people, it's worth examining before we move on.

Spiritual Frat Houses

Have you ever belonged to a fraternity? Its members have secret handshakes, inside jokes, matching jackets and a Latin name that's got to mean something wonderful. The frat brothers care about one another and cover one another's backsides. They eat, sleep, study, play and cause trouble together. I know that some awful things can happen in fraternities, but they certainly carry a sense of camaraderie and an atmosphere of brotherhood and loyalty to the group.

The members connect to a source of identity that's bigger than themselves as individuals, and they have a set of instant friends to help them navigate through those tumultuous college years. There's a satisfying feeling of security that accompanies enrollment, and assuming the newcomer can survive the hazing of induction, there is the potential for lifelong friendships. Fraternities become a type of family.

I never actually joined a fraternity like the kind I'm describing.

At least I didn't intend to.

I never learned a secret handshake—although I *did* join a group of people who spoke with some inside slang that an outsider would never understand. I never had an official club jacket—but I did look exactly like everyone else in the group. Our group didn't have a Latin name—but we sometimes referenced Hebrew and Greek words in our meetings. We never razed anyone who wanted to join—but it sure took an awfully long time for people to feel accepted, and some never did. I only wish we were more like a true family.

What do *spiritual* fraternities look like? You may have observed some different traits, but here are a few I've noticed.

1. Spiritual fraternities convey an attitude of elitism.

It's great to be on the cutting edge, and it's great to love your church. Some people forget, though, that the cutting edge is not quite as short as they think it is, and they forget that *a lot of other people are on it, too*. It's dangerous to believe that we or our church has a monopoly on a particular revelation or scriptural insight.

For years within one of my past churches, we spent considerable time and resources in reaching a particular group of people. Confined within the walls of our own congregation, we came to believe that we were alone, or cutting edge, or elite, in our efforts to minister in this specific way. After some time had passed and I had experienced a broader range of the Body of Christ, I realized that hundreds and even thousands of other churches were passionately ministering to the same area of society with an equally great fervor to see the Kingdom of God expanded there. How foolish it suddenly seemed to me that I had felt so superior in my heart.

Like the Lord had to remind Elijah, who once told God that he was the only faithful saint still alive in Israel, He had to say to me, too: "You're not alone—I have thousands of other followers who are pursuing Me with all of their hearts." A word like that certainly acts as a much-needed pinprick to a swollen spiritual ego.

2. Spiritual fraternities do not welcome different opinions or viewpoints.

One thing about my spiritual frat house was that we were always right. We just were. Sorry.

If someone disagreed with us, they were obviously a little less spiritually enlightened. If someone pointed out where we were in error, we naturally assumed that they had a bad attitude or a rebellious spirit. We didn't offer a platform for conflict resolution, and we didn't encourage differing opinions and viewpoints. Oh, we said that we did. We always said that everyone was welcome and that we wanted, even needed, their unique perspectives and insights. It's not that we didn't actually mean what we said—it's just that we should have added the disclaimer: *We want your input and opinions—as long as they agree with ours.*

I'm a little nervous about writing all of this because I don't want to sound too cynical and I don't want to be overly critical. I guess I can comfort myself, though, by the fact that you probably experienced some of this, too. Most of us who have spent any time around religious systems have encountered some of these dynamics. We're told to dream and be free, but when dreaming and freedom threaten the established structure, we've suddenly crossed the line into rebellion, and we're called "independent" and "troublesome."

Sometimes we *are* independent and proud and we must be open to correction and coaching, but for now, my point is simply to say that many wonderful men and women with strong leadership gifts are, at best, sidelined when they begin to speak their minds and, at worst, ostracized and intentionally shunned.

This should never happen in the Church.

3. Spiritual fraternities are full of cliques.

I want to be gentle with this point because I don't think people often *intentionally* act aloof and cliquish. I think they just love their circle of friends and, for whatever reasons, they sometimes make little or no effort to branch out beyond those relationships. Even though they are probably wonderful people, their disinterest in outsiders sends a clear vibe of the cold shoulder.

4. Spiritual fraternities are difficult to fit into.

It's tough to get into the inner circle of a fraternity, and in some churches, it's nearly impossible to break into the perceived inner circle. I say "perceived" because in any organization, there *will* be layers of relationship and trust, and these layers, or circles, are not inherently wrong.

It would be ridiculous to say that inner circles or special friendships are wrong—they're actually a part of the abundant life that Jesus promised us. The thing about Jesus, though, is that He was always willing to throw a lasso around other people and pull them into the loop.

He demonstrated this after His cousin, John the Baptist, was killed and He tried to withdraw for a time of rest and recovery with His own inner circle—the twelve disciples. They had been working so hard that they hadn't even had time to stop and eat, and they desperately needed a retreat. As they journeyed toward their anticipated haven, though, they saw a multitude of hurting people awaiting them, hoping for some touch or impartation of life. Instead of donning the fraternity jacket and closing the door to their needs, Jesus drew a bigger circle and invited them into their retreat.

I'm nowhere near where Jesus is. I'm not even on the radar of this level of love and compassion.

But I *want* to get there. I want to carry an atmosphere of "whosoever will, let him come." I want people to meet me and be undone by the love of Christ in me. I don't want to belong to a spiritual frat house. There were a couple of them in Jesus' day called the Pharisees and the Sadducees, and even our Lord Himself was excluded from them.

Let that never be us!

Now . . . before we make judgments about other people or churches, we need to search our own hearts—this is always wise when analyzing the strengths or weaknesses of others. Let's make sure that our own hearts are free from religion so we can model the amazing liberty that we have to pursue God with freedom and joy. If we do conclude that certain practices or groups of people are "religious," *let's not respond to them with our own religious spirit of judgment*. Rather, we should ask, "Is this something that is producing death and, therefore, something I should shun, or is it a tool in the Lord's hand to make me a more real, relational, effective leader for His Kingdom?"

Navigating topics like these isn't easy, but it is extremely important. The world is thirsting for life—for *the other life* that is awakened only by the reality of knowing God. Let's cleanse ourselves from any trace of a religious spirit. Let's repent of it and renounce and break its power by the authority of Jesus, so that we can say to the woman at the well that we, too, are carrying living water inside of us. Let's be like Jesus, who tore down religious temples and embraced the world in arms of love.

He can't stand religion, you know. In fact, the most hated king in the Old Testament was the one who ensnared God's people with a religious spirit. His name was Jeroboam.

God's Most Hated King

Almost everyone knows the story of how King Saul, the anointed leader of Israel, fell away from a true relationship with God and began to threaten the life of his successor, David. What fewer people know is that this identical story was played out between David's son, Solomon, and a younger man with David-like potential. In this story, King Solomon was God's anointed leader, but he began to worship foreign gods and give his heart away. Amid Solomon's spiritual decline, a young man named Jeroboam was distinguishing himself among the other men in Israel because of his excellent spirit and his industrious approach to life. Solomon was impressed with Jeroboam and brought him into his personal service; however, jealousy soon overcame him—like it had Saul, who had tried to pin David to a wall with his javelin—and before long, Solomon, too, began practicing his javelin-throwing skills on Jeroboam. To make a long story short, Solomon's family lost all but a tiny portion of the kingdom, and Jeroboam became the king of Israel.

These are startling similarities, aren't they? It's amazing to learn that Jeroboam, who had the potential to be another King David, became the most *hated* of all kings in the Lord's eyes. While David was known by God as the "sweet psalmist of Israel" (see 2 Samuel 23:1) and was the constant righteous standard by which every other king was measured, Jeroboam was the standard for anarchy and rebellion. The only other king to come close to him for his failure and sin was King Ahab—the king who invited Jezebel's terror into the land.

So, what happened to Jeroboam? What was the sin that so tarnished his legacy that when God judged future kings, He said that they did evil *like Jeroboam*? At first glance, it doesn't seem like what he did was all that bad. In fact, it almost seems as if he was trying to do good for the people of Israel. He tried to make it easier for the Israelites to worship

God by building high places where they could go without having to travel all the way to Jerusalem. It appeared fairly harmless at first glance—except that God hated the high places. God wanted to meet with His people in Jerusalem, but Jeroboam instituted a system that substituted religious observation for relationship. His decision was based on fear (as many religious structures are), and knowingly or unknowingly, he invited a religious spirit into Israel. The high places he built eventually became temples of idolatry, and every subsequent king was judged based on how they responded to them. Did they tear down the high places, or did they allow them to remain as a source of pollution in the land?

It's possible that we will be judged in that way, too. Did we tear down the high places of religion in our hearts and families and ministries, or did we allow them to remain?

I don't think that God is waiting for the day when we all don our spandex and pose for the world, but He does want us to live the message. He wants us to model what we're selling. He wants us to be relational beings who so exemplify the passionate, vibrant reality of life in His Kingdom that the skeptical onlookers sign up for what we're selling—just like I bought the Total Gym.

Questions for Consideration and Application

1. Is your religious service performed primarily in your own strength, or do you have the power of the Holy Spirit helping you?

2. Are you managing a religion or living in a relationship?

3. Has your religious experience become a duty, or is it a delight?

4. Have you ever acted as if you were part of a spiritual frat house?

5. Are you due for a special retreat where you reconnect with the lover of your soul?

13

A Leader Who Lost His Cutting Edge

In thee is rest which forgetteth all toil.

St. Augustine

Every now and then go away, have a little relaxation, for when you come back to your work your judgment will be surer; since to remain constantly at work will cause you to lose power of judgment.

Leonardo Da Vinci

Something attempted, something done, has earned a night's repose.

Henry Wadsworth Longfellow

Do you think of yourself as a leader? You are, you know. Oh, you may or may not oversee an organization or have hundreds of people following you, but you're still a leader.

The Bible says so.

The primary Hebrew word for *leader* has a fascinating aspect to its definition. In addition to meaning chief, captain and everything else that you would think the word *leader* might mean, it also means "a cloud or mist that rises up into the sky."[1] In other words, *leaders are those who rise to the top.*

I hope that's descriptive of you and me. Because we have the Spirit of God living inside of us, and because our seat at our Father's table is secure, we should *always* rise to the top. We should rise to the top in our homes and our relationships and our jobs—we should have the reputation of being those who always ascend.

I realize that this is easier said than done. I realize that all of us are probably already too busy and only getting busier and that it can be overwhelming to feel the pressure to always have to rise to the occasion. It's hard to always come through and be a Christlike example to everyone we meet. It's hard to keep the cutting edge in our lives—especially when we realize that the cutting edge is very easy to lose.

Have you discovered that the very things that first helped us achieve our edge are the things that eventually dull it? I gained a cutting edge as I got involved in Bible studies, Christian service, outreaches and conferences. I felt my faith growing sharper as I devoured dozens of books on the subject of spiritual growth and as I attended classes on theology and discipleship. My edge grew even sharper as I surrounded myself with accountability partners who would speak into my life and challenge me to continually grow and step into the ministry that the Lord had prepared for me. All of this activity was good for me and helped to fashion me into a man who had a cutting edge.

Unfortunately, the constant activity also eventually wore down that sharp edge.

We don't lose our edge during times of inactivity—we lose it during times of great usefulness and busyness. That's true of a natural edge, isn't it? I have a little pocketknife that I carry with me (my last one was confiscated at the airport when I had forgotten to pack it in my checked luggage), and I've noticed that its edge stays nice and sharp—as long as I don't use it much. However, when I carve a walking stick or open letters or use it for miscellaneous cutting tasks, it very quickly loses the edge that I so painstakingly scraped into it.

The same is true with our lives. It's not only possible to lose our spiritual edge, but it's inevitable. We *will* experience seasons when we lose the cutting edge—in our families, in our ministries and even in our relationship with God. When this happens and we feel a dullness settling over our lives, we should not panic and think that we're failing as believers, or even that we're backsliding in our faith. I've experienced these seasons of dullness and ineffectiveness, and I've almost always panicked.

I've questioned my devotion to the Lord, and I've questioned whether or not He should have ever called me into His service. I've felt like a fraud, and I have been sure that everyone around me could tell that I didn't love God as much as I had before. I hoped people couldn't tell how much I was struggling. You may have felt like this before, too.

When we hit these seasons of dullness, we need to remember that the Christian journey is not a sprint, but a marathon. Any lover of track and field knows that the human body can run at maximum speed for only 268 meters, and after that, no matter how physically fit the runner is, his or her body experiences a rapid deceleration. That's why races like the 400-meter dash are the most difficult in the sport. Every runner hits the wall—and the one who has the most gas left in his or her tank after hitting this wall is the one who will stagger victoriously across the finish line.

The author of the book of Hebrews said that we are running a race that has been marked out for us (see Hebrews 12:1). If we're running a race through life, we can be sure that there will be times of sprinting and dashing for all we're worth, but there will also be times of pacing ourselves and catching our breath. This catching our breath, the recovering of our cutting edge, is an incredibly important process—especially for leaders like you and me.

I've lost my edge as a parent before. As much as I adore my girls and hang on their every expression and word, there are times when I can feel my edge slipping. I'm still crazy about them, but I can feel an impatience surfacing in me. I become a little grouchier than usual, and I let them watch too many movies. It's not that I'm a bad dad; it's just that I need my space, and I'm happy to let them fend for themselves for a while. I'm present, but I'm absent all at the same time.

I've lost my edge in my marriage, too. I have the world's most amazing wife, and yet if I'm not careful, I can become more of a roommate to her than her lover. We can become ships passing in the night instead of ministry partners in life. We can pay bills and run errands and keep the house clean instead of sweeping each other off of our feet. We can begin missing one another in communication, and we can become touchy and overly sensitive.

I heard the story of a pastor who lost his edge in his marriage and almost didn't recover it. Fortunately, he saw the dullness settling over his relationship with his wife and determined to do something about it, so he reserved seats on a cross-country train ride. With nothing to do for several days but enjoy the scenery and one another's company, he and his wife boarded the train and settled in for the ride. He said that the ensuing awkwardness was the worst experience of his life as they both realized that they had lost their common interests and their ability to communicate. They were strangers—still committed and still concerned for the other's well-being—but merely going through the motions of love and life.

Fortunately for this couple, they recovered the wonder of their relationship. As the scenery raced by outside their window, they fell back in love, and they committed to never lose the edge in their marriage again. Unfortunately, many people have already lost it.

I've lost the edge in my Christianity at times. I think the times that I've been the most prone to lose it are when I forget that *I'm not only a believer, but an experiencer*. There is so much emphasis on believing God and believing *in* God that we can forget that the Bible was not given to us just so we could learn *about* God, but so we could engage in a passionate relationship *with* Him. We are experiencers. Yes, we believe in Him, but we are able to believe because we have experienced His presence and His voice and His character. Faith is never the result of a random choice to believe. Faith comes about only as a result of personally hearing the Word of God. We believe because we have experienced.

If it's been a while since you've *experienced* God, you've probably already begun to lose your edge. Hebrews 2:1 says that we need to pay close attention to the things we've heard and received "so that we do not drift away" from them.

I've caught myself drifting at times, and it's been only His divine rescue that has pulled me back on course.

I've been talking to a lot of people lately, and as we visit about life and God and how to grow and overcome, I keep coming back to the same bit of counsel for each person: When was the last time you took a day off of work just to be with Jesus? When was the last time you took a personal day just to worship and thank Him and meditate and recapture the wonder of being His child? Sometimes we must get off the treadmill and experience Him again. If we don't, it is inevitable that we will lose our cutting edge, and with it we will lose our passion, our effectiveness and, eventually, our joy.

There was a leader in the Old Testament who lost his edge. His story contains some wonderful counsel that can help us recapture ours:

> Now the sons of the prophets said to Elisha, "Behold now, the place before you where we are living is too limited for us. Please let us go to the Jordan and each of us take from there a beam, and let us make a place there for ourselves where we may live." So he said, "Go." . . . And when they came to the Jordan, they cut down trees. But as one was felling a beam, the axe head fell into the water; and he cried out and said, "Alas, my master! For it was borrowed." Then the man of God said, "Where did it fall?" And when he showed him the place, he cut off a stick and threw it in there, and made the iron float. He said, "Take it up for yourself." So he put out his hand and took it.
>
> 2 Kings 6:1–2, 4–7

Isn't it interesting that even a prophet can lose his cutting edge? Even a person who has a fresh, consistent word from God can grow dull. That encourages me. Let's examine a few thoughts from this passage that we can use as guideposts for recovering our own cutting edge.

The first thing I noticed in this story is that *their current home had become too small for them.* Your "home" is probably too small for you, too. I'm sure you know that there is more that you're called to—you haven't maxed out the Christian experience yet. There is more! You might be tired of hearing that—it might sound like the same old song that's been sung for as long as you can remember, but it's still true. There is more. There is always more in God. If it's been a while since you've experienced *more,* you may be in danger of losing your edge.

I like the fact that Elisha didn't rebuke the prophets when they said they wanted a bigger place. I think that God likes it when we come to Him and say that we're discontent and that we need more room to run. I think He wants us to dream and pray and live like He really is big and on our side.

So, they began a building campaign, and, verse 5 says, *"as one was felling a beam . . ."*

As one was living life . . .

As one was pressing in for a breakthrough . . .

As one was parenting his children . . .

As one was loving her spouse . . .

As one was fighting Goliath . . .

As one was felling a beam . . . the axe head fell into the water, and *he lost his cutting edge.*

Please notice with me that when the edge was lost, *the man didn't pretend that nothing was wrong.* He didn't keep swinging the handle in the hope that no one would notice what he had lost. He knew that living in denial never helps and that there is no sense in whistling in the dark. He knew—as you and I know—that once the edge is lost, the effectiveness is lost and all progress stops. So he cried out, "Alas, for it was borrowed!"

The lost edge was a borrowed edge. Isn't ours a borrowed edge, too? Doesn't our effectiveness in Christian service stem primarily from the anointing of Jesus Christ? Yes, we pray and practice the disciplines and do our duty, but *He* is the One who empowers us to do His work. We're not great, powerful saints all on our own—we're endued with *His* power, and it's *His* grace in our lives that enables us to overcome.

The wise prophet Elisha saw the plight of this younger man and prescribed four important steps for him to follow to recapture the borrowed edge.

First, he asked, "Where did it fall?" (verse 6). It's important for us to remember where we lost our edge. We need to think back to the last time we were overwhelmed with the wonder and awe of knowing Jesus. Where did we lose our edge? Where did the wonder slip out of our lives?

Second, the young prophet "showed him the place" (verse 6). Remembering is not enough—we have to ask the Lord to take us back to the place where we lost our passion and then ask Him to renew it. To the church in Ephesus, Jesus said, "Remember from where you have fallen, and repent and do the deeds you did at first" (Revelation 2:5).

Third, *God had to move*. This is my favorite part of the story. Elisha, obviously at God's prompting, threw a stick into the water, and the impossible occurred—the iron began to float . . . the edge was recaptured . . . the wonder was restored. I like this part because it reminds me that it's not up to me, all by myself, to recover the cutting edge. It's not up to me and my trying really hard to recover what I've lost.

There is a delightful worship song I heard recently that beautifully captures this concept. The young lady sang these words:

> I'll take my cold, cold heart,
> I'll take my unrenewed mind,
> I'll take Your Word in my hand,
> And then I'll give You time . . .
> To come and melt me.

She understands! She realizes that when the wonder is lost, there is only so much we can do ourselves. Yes, we must cling to His Word and do our best to remain faithful, but ultimately *He* must come in and melt us again with His love. Our job is to remain postured before Him—His job is to be God. The song goes on to say:

> Do what only You can do—come fan the flame!

I'll provide the tinder and the kindling, but *He* is the consuming fire that must melt me.

Are you okay with this line of thinking? Many of us have labored for so long under the tyranny of performance and the striving of works that it may seem strange to say that sometimes it's really up to Him. I'm certainly not advocating any form of abdication of our duty or responsibility—I'm simply saying that when the edge has sunk to the bottom of the river and there's no possible way we can dive deep enough to find it on our own, all we can do is trust that it was His edge in the first place and know that He will find it and return it to us.

This has happened to me countless times in my spiritual journey.

The fourth step that Elisha prescribed for the young man ties in well to the previous steps because, once God did what only He could do and the iron floated to the surface, the young man had to "put out his hand and [take it for himself]" (2 Kings 6:7). Yes, it's only God who can cause the edge to resurface, but once it does, we need to latch on to it with all of our might. It is a tag-team effort—God does the impossible and we respond in obedience.

Our church has adopted as a slogan, "We're all about The Presence!" because we recognize that the wonder is not recaptured or retained through human effort alone—we need to catch the wind of the Spirit in the mainsail of our lives. We need to be true to our nature as *experiencers*, not just believers. We need to stay postured as worshipers until *He* manifests His presence and we have no choice but to stand in awe.

We're all about The Presence. We need to be, because a poem and a principle don't cut it when the edge of our lives is sinking in the mire of a riverbed.

We're all about The Presence. We must be, because lost people can find religion anywhere, but what they really need is an encounter with a living God.

We're all about The Presence. It's essential if we're going to retain the wonder of our love for God, recapture the cutting edge when it grows dull and attempt to recover from the pain of the piercings that have tattooed our souls.

Questions for Consideration and Application

1. Have you lost the edge in any area of your life?

2. Are you convinced that you can get it back?

3. Has the busyness of life swept you into a frantic pace that makes it difficult to retain the necessary rhythm and balance of life?

4. What do you need to do to regain dominion?

14

MIMICKING GOD

What we love we shall grow to resemble.
Bernard of Clairvaux

To be loved, love.
Decimus Magnus Ausonius

Love spends his all, and still has store.
Philip James Bailey

I attended a delightful small-group meeting recently where a dozen of us had gathered in the home of a precious couple to visit, pray and study God's Word. When the time came to officially begin the meeting, the gentleman in charge did something a little unusual.

He opened his Bible to Ephesians 5:1 and read, "Be imitators of God." After that, he closed his Bible, looked everyone in the room in the eye and said three words: "Now . . . let's wrestle."

Some truths must be wrestled with. While there are some Scriptures that are so straightforward that we immediately understand them and move on, there are others that must be pondered, questioned, evaluated and wrestled with before their full revelation can be grasped. This particular Scripture, Ephesians 5:1, is one of those "wrestling verses." Let's climb into the ring together and try to get a choke hold on it.

Although it seems to be a simple text at first glance—it's just four little words—it is shockingly profound and extremely difficult to implement in our lives. "Be imitators of God."

What a statement! Be imitators of God. The verb tense used for this phrase is present imperative, which tells us that it isn't an invitation—it's a command that requires *full obedience* and must be carried out *now*.

Paul said, in essence, "I order you, right now, at this very moment, to imitate God."

That's a little overwhelming if you think about it. Imitate God?! How do we do that? The word *imitate* means "to reproduce or be the same as," or, literally, "to mimic."

My brother is a mimic. He's an actor who has starred in several Broadway plays and is currently filming a major motion picture. I've been watching him mimic different characters since we were kids in high school together, and I'm deeply impressed with his ability—but how does someone mimic *God*? How can we reproduce divinity?

Thankfully, we're not left to wrestle with these questions for long, because the next verse begins to provide our answer: "and walk in love" (verse 2). Imitate God—by walking in love. Can it really be that simple?

The word *walk* is a great word with a profound meaning. In the Bible it means "to regulate one's lifestyle." It doesn't mean to just scamper around on our two legs—it means that we are to regulate our entire lifestyles in such a way that *every aspect of who we are reflects love.*

We are told to make our way—the essence of who we are—*love.*

The ministry and mission of the Church can be summarized in one word: *love*. Where love is lacking, our greatest efforts at ministry are sterile and lifeless. Where love abounds, however, life is present. Christians who create an atmosphere of unconditional love and acceptance will bear fruit that remains.

In our attempts to win the world for Christ, we can never underestimate the incredible power of love. Love—manifested through kindness, the showing of preference, the expression of forgiveness, comfort, servanthood and unconditional acceptance—will melt resistance and will position people to encounter God.

Believers who genuinely demonstrate love contain more joy in their personal lives. They are freer and more secure. They are able to address a wider range of issues (including the confrontation of sin) while retaining the trust and loyalty of those around them. They also maintain a positive testimony with the world.

Life being as tough and challenging as it is, it's crucial that followers of Jesus provide a haven for weary souls. Just as Jesus manifested the love of the Father as He embraced sinners like Zaccheus, we must do the same to every person who graces our lives.

We exist to be expressions of the love of the Father to hurting humanity. Yes, we must confront sin and challenge people to grow, but we must always do so from a place of love.

I'm convinced that the primary search of mankind is not for doctrine, religious truth or strategies for successful living; it is for love. It is for acceptance. It is for belonging—and the world should find these in abundance everywhere a true Christian plays and works and shops and exercises and lives his or her life.

Two of our church elders (a beautiful couple who have been married for over forty years) serve as greeters every

Sunday morning, and as they stand at the door of our sanctuary, they convey the heart and love of God to everyone who enters. People have actually wept because of the love and warmth that they have experienced from this couple. People who encounter them have met Jesus long before we ever engage in praise and preaching.

I once asked this couple what their philosophy of ministry was. They responded: "We want everyone who walks through our doors to hear us convey the message: 'We've been waiting for you!'"

When people in the world see Christians who bear one another's burdens, who are quick to forgive, who fail to judge and criticize, who are quick to repent and ask forgiveness and who reach out with accepting arms of love, they will feel like they've come home. They will realize that they have truly encountered Jesus through our churches and ministries, and they will ask us the question, "What must I do to be saved?" When we as Christians walk in love, we will begin fulfilling the Great Commission of Jesus, and we will change the world. With love, we will become the sweetest sound on the planet; without it, we will simply be fingernails on a chalkboard.

Isn't that what Paul said? Doesn't the famous love chapter in 1 Corinthians 13 tell us that, apart from love, we are only a distracting irritation?

Christianity is all about serving people and imparting value and destiny to hurting and lost souls. Without these dynamics at work, we will never become all that God has intended us to be. At best, we will disseminate good information. At worst, we will be cold and lifeless.

I heard someone once say that the currency of earth is money, but the currency of heaven is relationships. I think that is true. It is the strength of our relationships that determines our success in Christian service.

The Lord not only wants to heal you from your hurtful experiences in church, but He wants to make *you* one of those saints "of whom the world was not worthy" (Hebrews 11:38). He wants *you and me* to mimic Him in front of our little corner of the world.

It's easier to do than you might think—even a child can do it. Or perhaps I should say *only* a child can do it. Paul said, "Be imitators of God, as beloved children" (Ephesians 5:1).

I wonder what was on Paul's mind when he pointed us to the nursery for our direction. What are some traits of children that can help us in our attempt at mimicking divinity? I'm sure there are a number of directions that this train of thought could go, but I think he might have been saying three things.

First, let's get back to the place where we color outside the lines.

Children never limit God, and I think Paul was exhorting us to return to the place where we dream big. I saw a humorous commercial on television the other day; it showed little kids who were daydreaming of their future. One boy said, "When I grow up, I want to file all day long," and the rest of the kids followed suit by longingly listing the menial, mundane things that they wanted to do with their lives. The humor in the commercial is the obvious fact that children *never* want to settle for mediocrity. They want to be doctors and firemen and ballerinas and astronauts and movie stars—and they usually want to be all of them at once! I think that *God has placed in the heart of every child a natural tendency to dream big.*

I heard of a study of creativity in people that tested levels of innovation in small children versus older adults. The findings were shocking as the study revealed that over 80 percent of children were extremely creative when they were five years old, but by seven years old—just two years later—only 10 percent of children still showed any significant signs of creative thought. The percentage went down to 2 percent by twenty years of age and stayed there throughout the rest of adulthood. The conclusion of the study was simply this: *As children are taught to "color within the lines," their ability to create and compose drastically diminishes.*

Paul said that we imitate God when we color outside the lines—when we think and dream big about what could happen if God really showed up.

Second, let's get back to the place where we are real.

Children are painfully transparent and real. Sometimes their transparency is cute and charming—sometimes it's embarrassingly direct. Our youngest daughter has recently won her battle with potty training, and now, whenever she has to go, she exultantly declares to everyone in the room, "I have to go potty!"

I'm not suggesting that we bare our souls with every person in every setting or situation, but I think that if we have erred, we've erred on the side of performance versus transparency. Christians should be the safest people on the planet with whom to bare our souls, confess our sins and find strength, healing and accountability, but unfortunately, most of us act like we're doing just fine. Because of this, we don't facilitate an atmosphere of safety for the person who *isn't* fine.

When there *is* an atmosphere of transparency, however, it can be deeply refreshing and liberating. I recently asked a man in our congregation how he was doing, and I received a very real response. He's a great man—a prayer warrior with a heart for the nations—but when I asked how he was, he replied with extreme honesty and vulnerability. "Not great," he said. "I was really discouraged last week, bought a half-rack of beer and got hammered, and now I'm trying to climb back out of the pit of condemnation."

I'm not condoning his discouraged actions, but I loved his transparency. He's the real deal—a very *human* being who is doing his absolute best to grow in Christ and impact the world. He's like the apostle Paul, who was striving for increasing holiness while battling an internal sin nature. We *all* have this rebellious sin nature to overcome, and if we would be more honest and transparent about our struggles, we would become a safe haven for those who are losing some of those battles.

Jesus was touched with every pain and emotion of humanity, and He never kept Himself aloof from the reality of life on planet earth. If we are to imitate God, we must do the same.

Every person who enters the sphere of our lives should see a passionate person who loves Jesus and who is doing his or her best to overcome sin and become more Christlike. The world should see someone who is transparent about the process and who is not presenting an "I've got it all together" façade. They should see children.

Third, let's get back to the place where we realize that we're His favorite!

That may seem like a strange thought, but it's very significant. When Paul told us to imitate God as beloved children, he was saying something wonderful about God's love for us. When Jesus was baptized by John, the heavens opened, and God the Father spoke audibly: "This is My beloved Son, in whom I am well-pleased" (Matthew 3:17). The word *beloved* means "favorite." He said, in essence: "This is My favorite Son!" We imitate Him when we realize that *we, too,* are His favorites.

I used to ask my mother who her favorite was between me and my brother and sister. She would always say, "You are!" I was so excited until I heard the same conversation play out between her and my brother. "Mom, who's your favorite?" he asked. "*You* are, son," she replied.

I do the same now with my girls. I tell both of them that they are my favorite—and they both believe me. They each know I tell their sister the same thing, but it doesn't change the revelation for them that they are Daddy's favorite.

The other day my eight-year-old daughter was telling me every minute detail of her day at school. As she repeated every word that had been exchanged by her and her play-mates at recess, I was so overwhelmed with love for her that I blurted out, "Amber, I could never tell you enough how much I love you!" She replied curtly, "Yeah, Dad, I know, but you're interrupting me." A beloved child should be so secure in her father's love that she never even questions the fact that she's adored. Both Amber and Madelyn are my favorite—and they know it.

It's extremely important that we grasp this revelation in our own lives. The world desperately needs to experience unconditional love and acceptance, but *we cannot export what we don't have*. If you and I don't know that we're His favorites, how will we ever walk a new believer into a reve-lation of God's endless love? First John 4:7–8 tells us that we can't really love others until we know God's love for us. However, if we know that we are a favorite child, we will acknowledge the favored status of others. This might be the first step to their reconciliation with God.

When Paul said to imitate God, I don't think he was say-ing, "Imitate Elohim—the One who set the cosmos in order." I think he was saying instead, "Imitate Jesus—imitate that aspect of His divinity that related to His Father as a favored Son." The overflow of their love was so profound that it drew the entire world into their relationship. Is *our* relationship with the Father doing the same thing?

Mine's not. But I want it to.

I desperately need more love. I need a deeper revelation of His love for me so that I can love others more, too. I need to care more for others than I do for myself.

John (who was nicknamed "the Beloved") spent more time with Jesus than any of the other disciples, and he wrote more about love than any of them did. I don't think it's a coincidence that the closer we get to Jesus, the more we hear about love. John captured Jesus' timeless words when He said:

> "A new commandment I give to you, that you love one another, even as I have loved you, that you also love one another. By this all men will know that you are My disciples, if you have love for one another."
>
> John 13:34–35

You're His favorite!

I hope you believe me. More importantly, I hope you believe *Him*.

One of my favorite thoughts from Scripture is found in Hebrews 13. The chapter starts out with the admonition, "Let love of the brethren continue." It then goes on to say that we should remember to be hospitable to strangers because in doing so we just might entertain "angels without knowing it" (verse 2). By continuing in love, we posture ourselves for angelic encounters.

We cry out to God: "I want to see angels! I want to meet Jesus!"

He responds: "Walk in love."

Questions for Consideration and Application

1. When people look at you, do they catch a glimpse of God?

2. Is love a top priority in your life?

3. When was the last time you "colored outside the lines"?

4. Do you believe that you're His favorite? You are!

15

BECOMING SOMEONE'S ANGEL

We are shaped and fashioned by what we love.
Johann Wolfgang von Goethe

To love is to find pleasure in the happiness of the person loved.
Gottfried Wilhelm von Leibnitz

Love comforts like sunshine after rain.
William Shakespeare

I met an angel once.

I was participating in a ministry trip to Slovakia in the mid-nineties when I received a memorable, life-changing lesson in humility. A precious older lady had graciously hosted me and my ministry partners, and she seemed incredibly honored to have us in her home. She was quiet, shy and unassuming, and I categorized her as just that: a sweet little old lady. It was fun to sleep in her guest room as the special visiting minister and to receive her respect and wonderful hospitality.

We visited briefly that first evening, and then I headed to my bed because a full day of ministry was planned beginning the next morning. But it was early in our European trip, and the time difference kept me awake for most of that first night in her home. I prayed for a few minutes and then lay there restlessly waiting for sleep to overtake my jet lag.

That's when she changed my life.

I heard her get up around 2:00 in the morning and walk into her kitchen. I wasn't trying to eavesdrop, but I was intrigued as I heard her begin to pray. I couldn't understand her words, but I could hear the desperate passion in her Slovak tongue. Her words began as a whisper but very quickly grew louder as her desperation overtook her. She worshiped. She wept. She cried out to the Lord on the floor of her tiny kitchen in the middle of the night, and from the brief language training I had received prior to our trip to Slovakia, I could tell that she kept saying, "Please, Lord! Please, Lord!"

She prayed for hours, and I lay in the other room realizing that *she* should have been teaching *me*. Indeed, she already was. I couldn't remember the last time I had prayed with that kind of passion or determination. As I listened to this sweet little grandma, I realized that there was hope for Slovakia.

When I saw her the next morning as she served breakfast to me and my partners, I couldn't help but ask her, "What were you praying for last night?" She had been praying for revival. She had been asking the Lord to visit her nation again—as she did every night. I flew back to the States, and she has since met Jesus in heaven. But what she did for me in those few hours was far more significant than anything I accomplished through my entire ministry in her nation. Someday in heaven, I'll thank her and tell her everything she meant to me. I'll probably have to wait in line to get to her.

I carry several thoughts with me now from my experience in her home. The first is that *I want to be her*. I want her passion and brokenness. I want the Lord to put His heartbeat in me—the way He put it in her as she travailed in prayer on her dark little kitchen floor.

The second thought is this: *What would happen if God answered her prayers?* What if He visited the nations with a sweeping revival? I believe it's His desire to do so. I believe that He wants to visit His people in such a way that the Church fully becomes everything He intended her to be and that society is reformed in the wake of His advance. I believe the United States is due for a third Great Awakening and that the other nations of the earth can also be transformed by a visitation from Him. I believe it even more as I remember that woman's prayers. As a church leader, though, I am constantly asking, *Are we ready?* When God moves in a significant way and thousands of people are born again, will we be ready to love them, heal them and help them to grow in Christ?

Another thought that I wrestle with is not just *what we will do when He answers our prayers for revival*, but *what if He decides to use* us *as the answer to these prayers?* It's a novel thought. What if God decides to answer our prayers for revival through Christians—through you and me?

That's been His pattern throughout history, you know. Despite His sovereign ability to do whatever He wants in the universe, and despite His ability to work signs, wonders and miracles in any situation, His primary means of answering prayer seems to be *through people*. If we read the Bible from a big-picture perspective, we will notice that when God answers prayer, far more often than He performs a miracle, He sends a person. *People* are the most common form of answered prayer.

Yes, God answered Israel's prayer and broke Egypt's back with all of the outrageous plagues He hurled on them—but it started with Moses speaking to a bush. A prayer went up from Macedonia—God's answer was the apostle Paul. When a certain man was robbed, beaten and left for dead on the road from Jerusalem to Jericho, the Lord didn't descend from heaven—He sent a Samaritan neighbor whom He knew would imitate God.

Think about your own life. When you are discouraged or hurting, God doesn't usually send an angel—He sends a note in the mail written by a friend who had you on his or her heart. When your children go off to college and begin to struggle with their faith, He doesn't usually appear in bodily form in their rooms—He schedules a believer to take the same class as they are taking and sit in the seat beside them.

Jesus called John the Baptist the greatest man born of a woman—not because of the miracles he did (to our knowledge he never performed a single miracle), but because he pointed people to Jesus. He got their attention, and then he showed them Christ—the true answer to their prayers. It's imperative that we do the same.

Have you ever thought about the fact that most answered prayers come in the form of other people? Of course, God can, and does, produce sovereign, supernatural answers to prayer at times, but very often, when someone cries to Him for help, *He answers through people.*

Years after my experience in Slovakia, I was perusing my journal, and I read an entry that I had written prior to that trip. In it, I was asking the Lord to increase my desperation and my burden for people. I had written out Jesus' words, that "blessed are those who hunger and thirst" (Matthew 5:6), and I was appealing to Him to increase my own hunger. As a comfortable American Christian, I had become far too satisfied. I didn't realize it at the time, but He answered that written prayer—not by sovereignly putting hunger in my heart, but by housing me with a little old lady who couldn't

LOVING GOD WHEN YOU DON'T LOVE THE CHURCH

sleep at night because she was so burdened by the condition of her nation.

I think God's first choice as a vehicle for answered prayer is His people. The scary thing about this is that *if we don't mimic Him well, the people who have prayed may never know that He's heard them.*

Answered prayer takes on many different faces. I can see them in my mind as I remember the times people have encouraged me—never knowing that they were the oracle of God for me in that specific moment.

One Sunday morning I was so discouraged that I didn't think I could cut it as a pastor. I didn't even want to be in church. I was still there, dutifully doing my best to lead and be a good example of devotion to the Lord, but I was hurting on the inside. I was feeling lonely and overwhelmed when I suddenly felt a gentle tap on my shoulder. I turned around and saw one of the men in our church holding an open Bible and looking at me with the most tender expression of love. He said, "God gave me this Scripture for you." It was an obscure one from Zechariah 2:4, and it read, "Run, speak to that young man, saying, 'Jerusalem will be inhabited without walls because of the multitude of men and cattle within it.'"

My friend had no way of knowing that I had been reading that same verse earlier that morning as I asked the Lord to strengthen me and speak to me about our church. I couldn't believe that the Lord would ask him to say to me, "Run! Encourage that young man!" He was the face of God to me. He was an answer to prayer.

I'm sure that, like me, you can remember multiple occasions when your church came through in a pinch and mimicked God well. I get to see it all of the time in my role as a pastor.

I recently visited an elderly lady in our church who had injured her leg and was in pretty rough shape. She couldn't cook, clean or even get out of her chair on her own. I had shown up at her apartment with my Bible in my hand, and I was ready to pray a fervent prayer of faith over her when I heard a slight commotion coming from her bathroom. I peeked around the corner and saw one of the younger ladies in our church on her hands and knees scrubbing the toilet. She smiled up at me as she cleaned, so I walked back to the living room and asked, "Has she been over here helping you a lot?"

My injured friend smiled and said, "Oh, yes, she comes over every day to help me. Some days she cooks, some days she cleans, and some days she just talks to me and prays with me."

I suddenly felt a little sheepish and realized that this young lady's cooking, cleaning and other practical help was far more a demonstration of the heart of God than any quick prayer that I could offer. I'm not belittling myself or my role there that day—I'm just keenly aware that one of the primary ministries of Christians is not merely to pray, but *to answer prayer.*

Let's be like my little Slovak angel.

Let's be like Jesus who was so secure in His Father's love that He was able to reach out to the world with an unconditional and endless love of His own (see John 13:1). When people leave our presence, let's cause them to say, "I've just encountered an angel, and my life will never be the same again."

Questions for Consideration and Application

1. Have you ever met an angel in disguise like the little old lady from Slovakia?

2. How did he or she impact your life?

3. Have you ever been an angel for someone else?

4. When was the last time you asked the Lord to use you to answer someone else's prayer?

16

TEN TIMES BETTER

If you saw how much work went into it, you would not call it genius.

Michelangelo

A hundred times every day I remind myself that my inner and outer life depend on the labors of other men, living and dead, that I must exert myself in order to give in the same measure as I have received and am still receiving.

Albert Einstein

What I'm saying to you this morning, my friends, is that even if it falls your lot to be a street sweeper, go on out and sweep streets like Michelangelo painted pictures; sweep streets like Handel and Beethoven composed music; sweep streets like Shakespeare wrote poetry; sweep streets so well that all the hosts of heaven and earth will have to pause and say, "Here lived a great street sweeper who swept his job well."

Martin Luther King Jr.

One of the most significant problems with Christians—*with me*—is that we so frequently surrender the image of God in us. Rather than living in our glory as the Creator's image-bearers, we live from our lower, natural selves. Consequently, instead of making creation do a double take when we walk by, because we look so much like God, we make them shake their heads in thoughtful disappointment. They wonder, *Is that what it means to be a Christian?* And they leave us in search of glory in another place.

Consider three thoughts from Scripture. In Genesis 1:26–28, God makes man in His image and then releases the dominion mandate to them, and He empowers Adam and Eve to take authority over the newly created world. Incidentally, the word *image* means to so closely resemble someone or something that you literally become the illusion of that person or thing. Adam and Eve looked so much like God that as they walked through the Garden, creation had to look a second time to realize who it was beholding. Was it God, or was it His son, Adam, or His daughter, Eve? We were made to look like God—and in that resemblance spread His fame throughout the world.

The second thought is from Daniel 1:19–20, in which King Nebuchadnezzar interviews candidates for his personal service. When he comes to Daniel and his three friends, the king discovers that:

> Out of them all not one was found like Daniel, Hananiah, Mishael and Azariah. . . . As for every matter of wisdom and understanding about which the king consulted them, he found them ten times better than all the magicians and conjurers who were in all his realm.

When Daniel and his friends walked in the image of God, they were found to be *ten times better* than the best the world could offer!

Now for the final thought. Proverbs 5 contains a wonderful exhortation from a loving father to his young son who is about to enter the turbulent period of adulthood. In it the father appeals to his son to forever embrace the way of purity and holiness and to avoid the "adulteress woman." Heed this counsel, the father said in verse 9, lest you "give your vigor to others and your years to the cruel one." The word *vigor* is an amazing word that means "splendor, majesty, excellence, brilliance and radiance"; in fact, everything about it points to *the image of God!*[1] *My sons and daughters, don't give away the image of God in you!* You were made to look like your Creator and to forever walk in the dominion, splendor and life of that image—don't surrender it! Don't give your splendor, your majesty or your brilliance away. He needs you—*the world needs you*—to look like Him. Creation is hungering for a glimpse of God—let it see Him *in you!*

Romans 8:19 tells us "the anxious longing of the creation waits eagerly for the revealing of the sons of God." Why? Not because these sons are so wonderful in and of themselves, but because they reflect His image. The world is hungering for God, and it hopes to catch a glimpse of Him in His sons and daughters.

This is where the conflict arises, because the creation that Paul referenced is *not* rocks and trees and mountains and streams—it is every person in every nation on planet earth. People are looking for their Creator—and they are supposed to find Him in us. The problem is that they seldom do.

In addition to the other areas that we have discussed so far, a major reason that people are leaving the Church today by the thousands is that *there is frequently no real discernable difference between Christians and the world.* We are *not* ten times better. Our marriages are not ten times better, our families are not ten times stronger and our businesses are not ten times more excellent. We're just like those of the world—and they aren't looking for their current level of power and life. They're looking for the glory of God.

Why should they come to our church? Why should they embrace our faith? Why should they allow us to teach their children and attempt to coach them on life? Oh, I know that *every* person should embrace our belief in Jesus so that they can live with Him forever in heaven, but there's got to be more *in this life*. Our faith in God *must* produce practical change in our daily lives or we are, at best, irrelevant and, at worst, a mockery. James said that faith without works is useless and dead (see James 2:17). What are the works of excellence and grace we perform that will prove that we are indwelt by God Himself?

I realize that I'm again painting with very broad brush-strokes. I know that I could enter every church in America and find people who are "ten times better" in many areas of their lives, but in general . . . we're not.

At least we're not in our marriages.

They say that the divorce rates within the Church equal that of the world—50 percent. No wonder we have no voice! If the world is looking for the splendor of God and all we can produce for them is a Christianized version of themselves, they will look the other way. *But what if we really were ten times better?* What if our marriages *were* ten times better than theirs?

If the success rates in marriage were ten times better in the Church than the world's 50 percent, *we could boast of a 90 percent success rate*. I can't say that we would reach 100 percent because there is, unfortunately, always room for the free will of man and the sin nature that assails us. However, we could say that the majority of true followers of Jesus will enter their twilight years with the glory of an untarnished marriage. If this were our testimony, perhaps the world would give us a voice. Perhaps they would seek us out, saying, "How can I have what you have?"

I've always thought longingly about the Scripture verse in which the unsaved people ran to the apostles, asking, "What must we do to be saved?" I've always prayed that I would have encounters like that. So, why don't I? I wonder if it's because no one sees anything in me that they think they need in their own lives. Of course, they do need salvation, but if they don't know about their need of the Savior, what else is there in me that would attract them to me—so that I could eventually tell them about their need for the Savior? I wonder what would happen if my life were ten times better. I wonder what would happen if Christians produced families that were ten times stronger than the best families in the world.

My hometown of Colorado Springs houses the ministry of Focus on the Family, and I frequently see a cynical bumper sticker that reads, "Focus on your own family!" I believe that Dr. Dobson and Focus on the Family are doing an outstanding job; however, there is still a mindset out there that says we have nothing that the world needs. *But what if we did?* What if our families were ten times stronger than those of nonbelievers? What if every household in our neighborhood saw the love, unity and life that exuded from us as we strolled around the block, and they realized that we had a glory that they have been looking for their entire lives? I think that if our families were consistently ten times better than theirs, people might start peeling those bumper stickers off of their cars and instead begin asking us, "What must I do to build a stronger relationship with my son . . . with my wife . . . with myself . . . with God?"

Imagine how prosperous Christians would be—and consequently, how financially sound churches would be—if all Christian business owners were ten times better than their competition. Imagine how many more referrals they would receive if the quality of their work and the level of their integrity were ten times better than those of anyone else in town. Imagine how many more raises and promotions average Christian workers would receive if their work ethic, attitude and level of excellence were ten times better than those of their colleagues. I think the word *favor* would soon become synonymous with *Christianity*.

Even better, if we followed Jesus' command and shined our light before men, they would see our good works and they would eventually meet and glorify their heavenly Father. This is what it means to be His image-bearers. Because God is a loving, *relational* Father at His very essence, *He has chosen to use sons and daughters who look like Him to bear His image and glory to the world.* He does this in such a way that unsaved people are attracted and inspired and drawn to Him. God has chosen His sons and daughters, *you and me*, to look like Him, and in the power of that resemblance, extend His Kingdom and win the world for His Son. We were made, first and foremost, to know our Father, to look like our Father and to spread the fame of our Father everywhere we go.

Now please don't get overwhelmed here. I realize that becoming ten times better may seem like a daunting task— but what about four times better? What about two times better? If we were to reread the Sermon on the Mount through this lens of "ten times better," we would see that everything about that exhortation was a calling for Christians to embrace the image of God. Everything Jesus said took the standard of the world and elevated it tenfold for His followers. He constantly said, "You have heard . . . but *I* say to you . . ." and then He raised the bar. Please notice that He didn't raise the bar because He wanted His religion to be difficult, overwhelming and ultra-spiritual—He did it because He knows that the image of God resides in every one of us and, just like the father in Proverbs 5, He pleads with us, "Whatever you do, don't relinquish the image of God that's been placed on the inside of you!"

He thinks you have what it takes to be the best. He thinks you have what it takes to be the light of your city and the salt of your world. He thinks there is greatness in you. He thinks there is excellence in you. Because you're His son or daughter, He thinks you have the potential to be ten times better. *He thinks His own nature resides in you.* He thinks you rock!

Look at what Nelson Mandela said about the image of God in you:

> Our deepest fear is not that we are inadequate. Our deepest fear is that we are powerful beyond measure. It is our light, not our darkness, that most frightens us. We ask ourselves, "Who am I to be brilliant, gorgeous, talented and fabulous?" Actually, who are you not to be? You are a child of God. Your playing small doesn't serve the world. There's nothing enlightened about shrinking so that other people won't feel insecure around you. We were born to manifest the glory of God that is within us. . . . And as we let our own light shine, we unconsciously give other people permission to do the same. As we are liberated from our own fear, our presence automatically liberates others.[2]

So how, then, do we begin to tap into this greatness? What can we do to begin looking more like the image we were made to reflect? How can we do a better job of representing Him in our churches and our world so that fewer people are disillusioned and hurt and more people are attracted to His brilliance? How can we keep from surrendering His image to the circumstances around us?

I have a simple thought to accompany these questions. I'm sure there are many ways to answer these questions, but I believe that one of the greatest ways to begin the journey toward "ten times better" is to *consistently make the right choice during defining moments.* It's during the critical moments of our lives that we either reveal or surrender the image of God in us.

During the defining moments of World War II, Sir Winston Churchill said this:

> The battle of Britain has begun. Upon this battle depends the survival of Christian civilization. The whole fury and might of the enemy must soon be turned on us. Hitler knows that he will have to break us in this island or lose the war. If we can stand up to him, all Europe may be free and the life of the world may move forward into the sunlit uplands. But if we fail, then the whole world, including the United States, including all that we have known and cared for, will sink into the abyss of a new Dark Age made more sinister, and perhaps more protracted, by the lights of perverted science. Let us therefore brace ourselves to our duties, and so bear ourselves that if the British Empire and its commonwealth were to last for a thousand years, men would still say, "This was their finest hour."[3]

Churchill believed that the deeds of a moment could define a millennium. If that is true, then certainly it's also true that the deeds of a moment can define a lifetime. Just ask King David, who took a walk on his rooftop at night, saw a woman bathing and, in a defining moment, chose to keep on looking.

What are defining moments? They include any moment—whether the midnight hour of World War II or a midnight stroll on a rooftop when Bathsheba is bathing—when our decisions will define our image.

The first step to becoming ten times better than the best the world has to offer—and thus spreading His fame throughout the world—is to choose, in every defining moment of our lives, to display the image of God. We must choose to be who we really are. When Christians give away the image of God, we become just like everyone else, and two things occur. First, we become salt without saltiness (like Jesus said in Matthew 5:13), and we become utterly unattractive to the

Loving God When You Don't Love the Church

world. The world already has "average"—why would they be attracted to more "averageness" in the Church?

The second thing that happens when we surrender the image of God is that the whole exhortation of being ten times better seems like an impossible pipe dream. After all, apart from Him, *we are the world*. However, when we cling to His image within us and rely on the Holy Spirit who indwells us, we become the answer for the world's search, and being ten times better becomes like kindergarten for us.

Whatever our calling, whatever our field, whatever our hurts, with all of our relationships and with every ounce of our ability, let's commit to choosing the image of God in us during defining moments and thus become the absolute best we can be. In that way, we will bear Him well to our corner of the world.

Questions for Consideration and Application

1. Do you know which aspects of the nature of God He has placed inside of you?

2. Are you walking in them?

3. Are you currently facing any defining moments in your life?

4. If so, are you intentionally choosing the image of God in the midst of them?

17

CHRISTIANITY DOESN'T MAKE SENSE WITHOUT IT

Great things are done when men and mountains meet.

William Blake

Servant of God, well done! Well hast thou fought the better fight.

John Milton

Doing little things with a strong desire to please God makes them really great.

St. Francis De Sales

The man who removes a mountain begins by carrying away small stones.

Chinese Proverb

Have you ever stood in front of one of those funky, psychedelic pictures that, at first glance, contains nothing but dots and designs, and yet upon further observation, reveals a hidden portrait? I've spent agonizing minutes at the mall trying to find the picture, hidden right in front of my eyes, behind the seemingly random pattern of colorful specks and dots. What I've found is that you can't see the picture if you're staring straight at it—you have to adjust your gaze slightly and almost look *through* the portrait if you hope to see its image. Sometimes that's a lot like life. Sometimes the answer is so close to us that we can't see it unless we adjust our focus and look from a different perspective. I know this is true of Christianity.

The Christian religion is a lifelong quest to know our loving Creator and become more and more like Him. We're constantly searching for more truth, more insight, more power and more life. We go to conferences, we stand in line for prayer and we attend small groups and discuss how little or how great our progress is. I do all of these things, too, so I'm not belittling them. I have bookshelves filled with notebooks and binders from conferences and seminars, and I have numerous covenant brothers with whom I divulge my failures and successes, but at the end of the day, I often wonder if I'm looking in the right places for answers to my questions.

I have quite a few questions. How can I know God more? How can I be more like Him? How can I prosper financially and thus bless my family? How can I be a better husband and father and ensure that those closest to me see a consistent example of Christlikeness in my life? These are important questions, and it's good that I'm taking them to church and accountability groups and conferences, but is there any other place I should go to find the answers? I want to experience the abundant life that Jesus promised me, but I often feel I'm living something that is, at best, good and, at worst, barely a trickle of life. Am I missing anything in my quest for life?

There is a young-adult leader in my church who likes to preach about the big picture of God's plan—the story He is telling through all of history and creation. As she was speaking one night, she told the audience, "Open your Bibles to the beginning of the story," so we all did as she asked. We opened our Bibles to Genesis 1:1, which starts out by saying, "In the beginning." She smiled knowingly and reminded us that Genesis 1:1 is the beginning of *man's* role in the story, but the real beginning of the story is found in John 1:1, which says, "In the beginning was the Word, and the Word was with God, and the Word was God." John 1:1 details the real beginning of the story.

Life doesn't begin with man, but with God. The story didn't begin when Adam and Eve pranced around naked in the Garden of Eden, but when the Trinity—the Father, Son and Holy Spirit—dreamed their family into existence and set in motion the creation of mankind. I was thinking about this one day, so I read the first chapter of John through the lens of the idea of origins. I mused that anything written at the very beginning of the story must contain great insight and relevance for those of us who are living out the story today. I also wanted to see if there was anything I was missing that could help answer my questions and lead me more fully into life. Sure enough, I found something.

In verse 14 of this chapter of origins, I read familiar words with a brand-new perspective: "And the Word became flesh, and dwelt among us, and we saw His glory." I've known about that verse for a long time, and I'm deeply grateful for that most awesome of miracles—Jesus, the Word Himself, becoming flesh and dwelling among us so that we could see the glory of our Father. But I read the verse differently that day. I realized that at the very beginning of the story, Jesus—the Pattern Son who sets the example for us in every area—established the fact that we, His followers, exist to wrap the flesh of our lives around the message of His Word and show other people His glory. Not only did *He* become flesh and dwell among us, but *we* are to be the flesh-encased word that shines so brightly among those around us that people behold the glory of God.

If any project, process or expedition gets too far away from its original design, it is destined to fail. If our Christian religion gets too far away from this foundational truth of why we exist, it will eventually fail us.

The great story of life begins with the Word becoming flesh. The Church began the same way. Think about Jesus' final commission to His followers when, in Matthew 28:19, He set the course for the Church through the ages. He said, "Go therefore and make disciples of all the nations, baptizing them in the name of the Father and the Son and the Holy Spirit." When He said this, He must have been thinking of the ages He spent with the Trinity, as they dreamed of the Word becoming flesh so that a family of sons and daughters could see the glory of God and make their eternal home with Him. He must have been remembering the purpose of the story when He told His followers, in essence, "Go therefore and wrap the flesh of your lives around the imperishable Word so that mankind will again behold the glory of their Father and turn to Him."

The religion of Christianity was birthed out of this mindset of the Word becoming flesh. *Christianity, as a religion, was spawned in the context of mission.* If we ever separate it too much from this early mandate, it will stop making sense, and eventually it will not work. Oh, it may work for a while. Good, solid principles will always bear fruit if you apply them—but the Christian life is about far more than following good principles. A Buddhist who practices honesty will reap the fruit of honesty, and a Muslim who practices moral purity will reap the benefits of moral purity; however, these principles alone will never lead us to life. Jesus said of the Pharisees that they searched the Scriptures in pursuit of life, but they couldn't find it. *They could not find true life because their religion had become divorced from mission.*

Has yours?

I know we're discussing our need to receive healing and refreshing from the bruising we've received within the four walls of the church, but we have to do more than that. The answer is not just to get healed from the hurts caused by the church, but for us truly to *become the Church*. I don't mean for us to become the Christian religion. Religion in any form—be it Islam or Buddhism or Christianity—is bondage. Jesus came to bring us life, but the life He promised us is shrouded in the context of mission.

On days when I share my faith with an unsaved person, I am on top of the world. When I truly sprinkle a little salt and light in my neighborhood, I feel so good inside that it really doesn't matter if other Christians are petty and spiteful. The sense of mission reminds me that I am part of a bigger story and that I have a bigger role to play than just that of a regular churchgoer. I exist to manifest the glory of God! I exist to wrap the flesh of my life around the Word, the Logos, the essence of God, so that my brothers and sisters here on earth can see the glory of God. When I do this, I regain perspective, and my religion again makes sense.

The other night I attended a class at our church—actually, I taught the class—and I had a good time. I shared some interesting truths from the Bible, and I think I blessed the people who were in attendance. Of course, they're just like me—they're looking for more life than they have, and they were hoping that my talk would help them find it. Anyway, I left the class and headed to my car with a mild sense of satisfaction. When I got outside, though, I had an experience that far exceeded the joy of merely teaching a Bible study.

There was a young man walking back and forth outside of our church, peering intently into the windows of our building. I introduced myself to him and asked him if I could help him find anything. He extended his hand to me, looked at me with very intense, clear eyes and said, "I was just wondering what was going on in there." I explained to him that we were having a church service and teaching our men how to be better husbands, fathers and leaders so that we would leave a positive impact on our world. He smiled in affirmation, so I asked him, "Are you a Christian?" He replied, "Oh, no. I am a Muslim, and I was just walking and praying and wondering if there was a reason that I passed by this church."

We talked and exchanged phone numbers, and then committed to meeting for further discussion. Although I didn't lead him to Christ, I felt more alive than I had felt in ages— because I was engaged in the mission. I had done my best to reveal the glory of God that was inside me. I eventually told him, "I think there was definitely a reason that you found our church and met me."

I'm convinced of it.

Please hear my heart. I'm not downplaying the crucial role of ministry within the Church, but I am trying to remind us that our faith will work only in the context in which it was birthed. And that context was mission.

When was the last time you intentionally shared your faith? When was the last time you awoke in the morning and said, "Father, thank You for the awesome power You have deposited into my life—now, who needs to be set free today? Who needs to experience the love of God today? Where can I release Your glory today?"

I'm not saying that the answer to all of our searching is witnessing and soul-winning, but I am saying that if we get too far removed from the origins of our faith, it stops making sense. Remember, Christianity is not about us. When we strive to find our lives we will lose them, but when we live to give as much life away as possible, we enter into life like we've never known before—the very life of Christ.

Some things will never make sense for us apart from a sense of mission. Many things will never make sense apart from the presence of God. Asaph, a worship leader in ancient Israel, wrestled with this. In Psalm 73 he revealed what he had learned.

He knew that God was good . . . but he was baffled by all of the contradictions and paradoxes of faith. For example, the wicked prospered, the boastful were secure in their strength, the ungodly were at ease as they increased in their wealth and those who mocked God were so blessed that they had more than their hearts could wish for.

For Asaph, however, he felt he had washed his hands in vain. He felt he had kept a pure heart for nothing, and for all of his devotion, he was plagued and chastened every morning. None of this made sense to him until he reached verse 17. At that point he finally said, "Until I came into the sanctuary of God; then I perceived."

Life makes no sense . . . until we return to the sanctuary of God. Christianity makes no sense . . . until we return to the place of mission.

Questions for Consideration and Application

1. Has your Christian religion become divorced from the mission in which it originated?

2. When was the last time you intentionally engaged in the mission?

3. Are you willing to wrap the flesh of your life around the Word of God so that someone else can behold His glory?

LOVING GOD WHEN YOU DON'T LOVE THE CHURCH

18

THE 21ˢᵀ-CENTURY CHRISTIAN

Cowards die many times before their deaths; the valiant never taste of death but once.

William Shakespeare

We must engage in the spiritual battles of our own generation.

Martin Luther

*D*o *what the occasion requires!*
What a great statement! It's an inspiring command that is especially relevant to believers in Christ today as we face a culture and society that is bent on derailing the Kingdom of God and establishing an anti-Christ agenda in the earth.

Do what the occasion requires! This statement comes from the Bible, from the passage when the prophet Samuel gave this command to the newly anointed King Saul. Samuel told Saul that the Spirit of the Lord would come upon him and he would prophesy. He would be changed into a new man and then, in the strength of that anointing, he was to *do what the occasion required* (see 1 Samuel 10:7).

I love that verse!

The occasion of the 21st century requires a specific response. It requires a specific breed of Christians. The day and age in which we live requires a specific type of church. We in the 21st century face challenges and crises unknown to former generations, and we must be equipped to respond according to the need of the day. If we fail to respond to the occasion, we leave it to our children and grandchildren to face the giants that we ourselves should have slain. We leave well-established societal strongholds for them to grapple with when we could have torn them down in their infancy. We must do what the occasion requires!

The good news is that God has known all along what the specific challenges of each era would be, *and He has strategically placed believers in those eras to respond to them.*

The words of Mordecai to the frightened Jewish Queen Esther are still true for us today: "And who knows whether you have not attained royalty for such a time as this?" (Esther 4:14). What is *a time such as this?* George Barna describes our time as follows:

> The Church in America is losing influence and adherents faster than any other major institution in the nation. Unless a radical solution for the revival of the Christian Church in the United States is implemented soon, the spiritual hunger of Americans will either go unmet or be satisfied by other faith groups.
>
> Within the next few years, America will experience one of two outcomes: either a massive spiritual revival or total moral anarchy.[1]

I personally believe that revival is coming. I don't believe it is coming just because it's coming—I believe God is looking for true Christians who know that they've come into the Kingdom for such a time as this. They will pray like Daniel as they contend with false ideologies; they will raise godly families with true, biblical worldviews; and they will model holy lifestyles that carry the presence and power of God. Paul said that creation itself is longing, literally groaning as in the pain of childbirth, for the revealing of such sons and daughters (see Romans 8:19–22).

I believe he was talking about *you*.

God knew what challenges the 21st century would hold, and He knew what the occasion would require. The occasion never takes the Lord by surprise.

When God was master-planning the redemption of mankind, He knew exactly what the Church would face in each century. He knew all about the first-century persecution of Christians. He knew about the Dark Ages and the Middle Ages. He knew about the Edict of Worms that Martin Luther would challenge. He knew about the sexual revolution of the 1960s that would capture the heart of a generation. He knew that prayer would be taken out of America's public schools and that abortion would be legalized in 1973.

He knew we would be living to see the first legalized gay marriages in America.

He knew our children would grow up in a culture in which MTV vies for their hearts and in which the pressure to conform to immoral standards would be unprecedented.

He knew we would be raising our families in a society in which the prevailing worldview is postmodernism (the existential movement that stresses the exercise of free will in a purposeless universe; the belief that there is no destiny, no absolutes, no loving Creator and, consequently, no true hope).

He knew we would face an enemy that was determined to undermine and obliterate God's standards for life, happiness and fulfillment.

He knew all of this, and He knew that to combat the world powers of this day, He would need a certain breed of Christian. In other words, He would need heroes. Knowing all of this, when He looked down through the ages and realized that you would respond to the grace of salvation, *He chose to plant you in the 21st century.*

He looked into your soul and your spirit, and He saw the stuff of an overcomer. He saw the stuff of champions. He saw the grit and tenacity of a martyr. He was looking for a champion, and He knew He had found one in you.

He believed that deep inside, you have what it takes to do what the occasion requires.

Don't be overwhelmed by all of this. It's okay if you don't feel like a conquering hero right now. As always, God gives us a pattern to follow, and in this case, it isn't an unrealistic one.

The book of Judges tells an obscure story of a man named Ehud who, despite extreme personal brokenness and heartache, became a hero who brought peace *to two consecutive generations.*

The story of Ehud is a calling for champions, but it isn't an unrealistic, unreachable story. Ehud didn't have it all together, and he certainly wasn't perfect. He was a heartsick hero—a hope-deferred champion. He was a lot like you and me. The only real strength that he possessed was that he stayed in the Lord's presence until God's heart was formed in him *and until he received a message from God.* His prayer was "God, make me the message!"

One of our elders recently asked several profound questions of our ministry team: "What is your message? And is it packaged in your life?" Ehud embodied his message. Here's his story. (You can read it in its entirety in Judges 3.)

A new generation was arising in Israel when an enemy king named Eglon emerged to oppress them. The name *Eglon* means "to encircle or surround," and he oppressed Israel with a tenacity that matched his name. They felt encircled by him—everywhere they turned, he was there. They couldn't get away from him.

He was a fierce, aggressive enemy king, and for eighteen years, his iron yoke of oppression had enslaved an entire generation in Israel. The people were in need of a champion, and when the Holy Spirit called for a hero, Ehud stood to his feet.

He wasn't a likely choice for a hero, though. He was from the tribe of Benjamin (which means "the son of my right hand"), and yet Judges 3:15 said that he was a "left-handed man." Many Bible scholars and commentaries suggest that this means Ehud wasn't simply left-handed—as opposed to being right-handed—but that he was actually crippled in his own right hand. In other words, he was a walking picture of tragedy. He was injured in the very area of his destiny. He was lame in the area of his greatest strength. How embarrassing it must have been for him. "You're a Benjamite—a son of the right hand? You can't even use your right hand—how can you ever hope to wield a sword and deliver Israel?"

Ehud didn't need Eglon's iron yoke to encircle him in order to feel oppressed—he faced enough internal oppression to keep him bound and discouraged. The people did not view him as a deliverer. In fact, when the king demanded a tribute from them, they nominated Ehud to carry the gift to the ruler, thinking that a crippled man might elicit sympathy from the evil king. What a pitiful picture of the condition of the nation of Israel: "Let's send a broken man to carry our peace offering to our enemy."

There was something special about that particular broken man, however, because his name meant "joined together."

Ehud had so joined himself together with the heart of God for his generation that, according to Judges 3:15–16, while the others prepared a tribute, he prepared a dagger. He fashioned an eighteen-inch double-edged knife that he strapped to his thigh with murderous intent. The King James Version of the Bible says that he "made him a dagger." Yes, he prepared a deadly blade, but he also made *himself* into a weapon so that while others assembled the tribute payment, he prepared the death sentence of the king.

While the children of Israel wondered, *How can we appease our oppressor?* Ehud thought, *How can I bring him down?*

We must think the same way.

We can't simply coexist with the ideologies of our day. We can't peacefully allow our nation to be overrun and destroyed by demonic strategies. Instead, we must be like Ehud. We must get in the presence of the Lord until we receive a word and *become the message*.

The climax of Ehud's story took place after he gave the tribute gift to the king and asked for a word with him in private. He and the king stepped aside into a secluded chamber where Ehud said, "King, I have a message from God for you." Then he whipped out the eighteen-inch dagger from beneath the robes over his right thigh and plunged it into the king's stomach until the blade protruded from his back and lodged immovably in his midsection.

The rest of the story, as they say, is history. Ehud galvanized the people of Israel into an army and then routed Eglon's forces, breaking forever the encircling grip he had held over the nation and inducting a two-generation era of peace and prosperity in the land.

We need a message for the world. We can't try to step in and compete with the world's system on its level. We need to be given an errand that comes from the secret place.

God has never called the Church to entertain the soul. He's never called the Church to tantalize the intellect— He's called it to enforce the rule of a King. A. W. Tozer said that "the message of the gospel is not a compromise but an ultimatum."

To be a relevant Christian in the 21st century, we must have something that transcends the world. We must have something that supersedes psychology and humanistic attempts to become good, whole people.

The 21st-century Christians are on a mission from a King. They are pilgrims on this earth with a secured citizenship in heaven and a desire to make their lives count for God.

One of our identifying marks must be a message from the heart of God. What types of messages does the world need to hear? How about the message that God isn't mad at them but that He's been pursuing them from the foundation of the world? How about the message of reconciliation with God and other people?

How about the message that the loose ends of our Christian faith will not strangle our destinies and that our brokenness will be used as a weapon? How about the message that MTV will not steal the heart of this young generation and our nation will not sink into further apostasy?

What are some of the specific messages that *you* were meant to carry? What areas of brokenness in your life does God want to forge into a weapon? I don't know. That's part of your assignment from God to discover.

"I have a message from God for you."

Can you say that? He's looking for men and women who will become the message and will drive it into the heart of His enemies.

He's calling for a deliverer. He's calling for a hero.

I'd like to conclude this chapter with an essay that I read years ago entitled "My Colors." I've never been privileged to know the author's name, but I have been blessed repeatedly as I've read it many times and allowed it to penetrate and convict my soul. It summarizes perfectly the marks of a 21st-century Christian.

My Colors

I am part of the Fellowship of the Unashamed. I have the Holy Spirit's power. The die has been cast. I have stepped over the line. The decision has been made. I am a disciple of Jesus Christ. I won't look up, let up, slow down, back away or be still. My past is redeemed, my present makes sense and my future is secure. I am finished and done with low living, sight walking, small planning, smooth knees, colorless dreams, tame visions, mundane talking, chintzy giving and dwarfed goals.

I no longer need pre-eminence, prosperity, position, promotions, plaudits or popularity. I don't have to be right, first, tops, recognized, praised, regarded or rewarded. I now live by presence, lean by faith, love by patience, lift by prayer and labor by power. My pace is set, my gait is fast, my goal is heaven, my road is narrow, my way is rough, my companions few, my guide reliable, my mission clear. I cannot be bought, compromised, deterred, lured away, turned back, diluted or delayed. I will not flinch in the face of sacrifice, hesitate in the presence of adversity, negotiate at the table of the enemy, ponder at the pool of popularity or meander in the maze of mediocrity. I won't give up, back up, let up or shut up until I've preached up, prayed up, stored up and stayed up the cause of Christ.

I am a disciple of Jesus Christ. I must go until heaven returns, give until I drop, preach until all know and work until He comes. And when He comes to get His own, He will have no problem recognizing me. My colors will be clear.

**Questions for Consideration
and Application**

1. Do you believe that God has strategically placed you in this hour of church history?

2. Do you believe that, in Him, you have what it takes to do what the occasion requires?

3. Like Ehud, are you willing to be used by God despite your pain and wounding?

4. When was the last time you heard a message from the secret place? God is waiting for you there!

19

THE 21ST-CENTURY CHURCH

It is not fitting when one is in God's service, to have a gloomy face or a chilling look.

St. Francis of Assisi

Alexander, Caesar, Charlemagne, and myself founded empires; but on what foundation did we rest the creations of our genius? Upon force. Jesus Christ founded an empire upon love; and at this hour millions of men would die for Him.

Napoleon Bonaparte

I would like to include a chapter here that slightly detours from specifically discussing you and me as individual believers and instead focuses briefly on a bigger picture of the Church. As we move past the hurts we received in church and resolve to take our place again in God's plan for His Body, it's important to recognize what that plan is so we can identify what our role in it might be.

I think I can safely say with great accuracy that the place and purpose of the Church has *never* been more critical in the history of America than it is right now.

Jack Hayford, pastor of The Church On The Way in Van Nuys, California, recently said that we are entering the *hour of the Church*. He said:

> I predict the coming century to be one in which a clear concept of the Church, her mission and her truest, timeless and most effective strategies will be regained. As I look across forty years of pastoral leading, and then scan the present horizon of the Church in ours and other nations, I perceive "an hour" has arrived. It is an hour of citywide impacting that is beginning to occur in New Testament ways, because New Testament vitality and spiritual penetration is taking place. In this hour the Church has become less enfranchised by society's institutions; she is becoming more effective in her impact.
>
> Jesus laid the truth before us long ago: His Kingdom will never gain high currency with any contemporary culture in terms of power, control or economic dominance. But if she is alive and well, His Bride will multiply children everywhere, until the salt flavors the world around it, and the light beams ever more deeply into blinded souls and steadily shines in the face of evil's surrounding darkness.[1]

The church is *not* irrelevant! We may have become so in certain areas, but God wants to visit His Church again, and as moral darkness increases, He is bent on baptizing it with increasing purity and power. He's looking for congregations who will *do what the occasion requires.*

What do these congregations look like? What pattern can we follow in order to grow into these culture-shaping congregations? There were actually many great churches in the New Testament to which we could look for insight.

The church in Ephesus was very significant. It functioned in a city that contained a 50,000-seat theater and the temple of Diana (one of the Seven Wonders of the World), and it was one of the most influential cities for the international spread of the Gospel.

The evangelistic church in Philippi was strategically stationed at one of the main east-to-west crossroads where merchants and traders traveled on the great Roman highway.

The church at Colossae became a bastion of truth against an influx of new-age philosophies and indulgence in astral powers. The culture of Colossae was rampant with Gnosticism, that philosophy that elevated knowledge and reason above all physical matter. It propagated immorality and unrestrained sin because Gnostics believed that all physical matter was inherently evil and had no bearing on salvation anyway. The church in this city stood as a champion of the faith amid a backsliding culture.

What about Thessalonica? The church in this city was Paul's crowning achievement. This church contained the greatest number of believers, had the most social respect and continued to grow and thrive even though Paul felt that he had not had adequate time to ground the believers fully in the faith.

All of these and other New Testament churches, like the one at Jerusalem, contain great insights from which we could glean deep truths, but I think that out of all of them, one stands out as a picture of what our culture really needs today—the church in Antioch. This church is a perfect model of what heartbroken Christians are looking for and of what desperate unbelievers really crave. If Antioch existed in our cities today, the lost would flock to its doors and disillusioned saints would feel that they had finally come home. Love so permeated the lives and gatherings of the saints that *the world—the unbelievers—named them "Christians" there.*

Acts 11:26 says the believers were "first called Christians in Antioch." Antioch was the first church to inspire the name "Christian." It has been commonly taught, and you have probably heard it, too, that when the disciples were dubbed "Christ-ians," it was with an attitude of ridicule and scorn. The unbelievers jeered them and mockingly named them after their crucified leader. Although it is true that there was this element of mockery in the naming, it's also true that *there must have been something in the believers that made the world think of Christ*—somehow the disciples reminded people of Jesus.

Something else fascinates me about this identification. This incident of believers being "called Christians" is actually an example of God using unbelievers to speak the prophetic word of the Lord. The word *called* means "to speak as a divine oracle." It literally means "to be sovereignly led to speak a word from God."[2] The word was used in the story of the magi when they were warned in a dream not to return to King Herod after they had seen the baby Jesus (see Matthew 2:12)—it means to experience a sovereignly inspired change in course or direction.

In Numbers 23, Balaam, who had been hired to curse Israel, said, "How shall I curse whom God has not cursed?" (verse 8). This is exactly what happened later in Antioch. The antagonists of the disciples, in their attempt to curse and criticize, ended up blessing the believers' destinies: "You're Christians. You look like Christ!"

The root word, *chrio*, from which the word *Christian* is derived, means "to anoint." The cynics in Antioch actually said, "I'm trying to curse you, but all I can say is, 'You are little replicas of the Anointed One!'"

Today, the Church is trying to tell the world who we are—but I'm longing for the day *when the world tells us who we are*! I'm longing for the day when unbelievers say, "You're Christians, aren't you?" I'm not waiting for them to say, "You're a churchgoer, aren't you?" or, "You're a spiritual nut," but, "You're anointed—and the anointing stirs some-

thing deep in the core of me. *What must I do to be saved?*"
You remember that they asked that question in the early
days of the Church, don't you? (See Acts 16:30.)

Antioch changed the world. It was from this place that
the Holy Spirit commissioned Paul and Barnabas to do the
work that He had called them to do. Paul had been called
while on the road to Damascus as a "chosen instrument" to
bear God's name before the Gentiles (see Acts 9:15), and
seventeen years later *in Antioch*, he was finally and fully
commissioned to pursue that calling. Antioch was a place
where lifelong callings were finally commissioned.

What would we see if you and I were able to time travel
to this first-century city? What would a week in Antioch
look like? Who would we encounter? What would the atmosphere in the church be like? I think that if we could don
our sandals and follow Paul and Barnabas around in Antioch
for a week, we would notice seven different characteristics
of this body of believers. (Note: For a full biblical study, you
can find these seven traits in Acts 11 and 13.)

1. Broken believers make their way to Antioch.

Many of the believers in Antioch had been "scattered because of the persecution" (Acts 11:19). The word *persecution* is
a brutal word that means "to break by squeezing."[3] The picture
is of an object that is being forced down an increasingly narrow
tube. The pressure from the collapsing tube becomes so great
that the object eventually cracks, breaks and finally crumbles
into tiny pieces. Wow! I feel as if I have just described some
of the seasons in my past—probably yours, too.

The pressure of the persecution in the first century had
broken these believers and scattered them. The word *scattered*
used in this verse was a farming term that usually referred to
a sower who scattered his seed. I like that idea—Satan was
trying to scatter the believers, but God was actually sowing
them as His seeds!

I wonder if it's possible that the Lord has planted you where you are. I wonder if it wasn't an accident that you've arrived in your current location. Maybe you feel as if the devil has scattered your hopes and dreams and that you've arrived where you are by hardship, squeezing and pressure, but perhaps God has "sown" you there because He believes you can bear fruit in your current assignment.

Even though God may have been behind the scattering of those early Christians, they had still been persecuted—and it was *broken* believers who made their way to Antioch. Broken believers have made their way to every church in our nation—it's a smart move on their part. When life has crushed their dreams, where else should they go? They should go to the place that is said to offer answers, hope and reviving—they should go to the Church: the house of God.

Let's be very sensitive and gentle as we relate to our fellow believers—they may be feeling broken and scattered inside their souls. They might look fine on the outside—many people are masters at "faking it"—but they may be desperate for a glimpse of life. They may have a sign over their hearts that echoes the words of the Traveling Wilburys, Roy Orbison and Bob Dylan's group from the 1980s: "Handle me with care."

People in Antioch aren't intimidated by brokenness. It doesn't make them uncomfortable, because they've lived through their own persecution and they are quick to embrace those who have been scattered.

In 1990, I experienced a season of brokenness that left me feeling dazed and scattered. On the heels of this scattering, I drifted into a church that, for me, was Antioch. I had gradually moved away from God, and although I knew that only He could fill the gaping hole in my heart, I was clueless about how to find Him again. Thankfully, I found believers who themselves had drifted and then been moored back into the grace and love of God. They latched on to me. They embraced me. They trained me, and they befriended me. Ten years later, they ordained me and commissioned me to the work that God had called me to do. I felt like Saul, who before was a blasphemer and then had an encounter with God, experienced a name change, underwent a season of preparation and, finally, was commissioned into God's service.

Broken people make their way to Antioch. There's another dynamic that occurs there, as well.

2. Barnacles come off in Antioch.

Barnacles are fascinating creatures. They are crusty, little marine animals that attach to hard surfaces. Their teeth excrete a chemical that dissolves shells and rocks and the tough skin of whales and, literally, cements them to hard surfaces. They are sturdy and sharp and nearly impossible to remove.

Did you know that you're carrying some of these sharp edges? I am, too. And we bring them right into the middle of our Antioch. In hard seasons of scattering and brokenness, barnacles attach themselves to our lives, and we carry them with us everywhere we go.

The funny thing about these barnacles is that we can spot them immediately on the people around us, but they are nearly impossible to detect in our own lives. We get hurt and cut by the believers around us, but we fail to notice that we have some defense mechanisms of our own. We can accurately discern the issues in our church, but we miss the fact that when people get too close to us, we can cut them to ribbons, too. Other people's barnacles hurt us—and ours hurt them.

Brokenness is a good thing. The brokenness I've experienced has produced a level of humility in me that I never could have received any other way. I cherish brokenness, and I always want my life to carry the scent of it. However, along with this fresh dose of humility, I also inherited a batch of ugly—and dangerous—barnacles. Be warned—if you approach me from the wrong angle, I might scrape the skin right off you.

Barnacles come off in Antioch. They have to because, when left unchecked, they will render us ineffective.

As great as it was, the church in Antioch had a barnacle problem: The broken people who had been scattered there would speak to only their fellow Jews. They had been scattered because of persecution from the Roman Empire, and in the wake of that pain, barnacles had attached to their brokenness—and they refused to speak to Romans. They thought, *I've been hurt by a Roman before—so I'll shut myself off from all Romans everywhere.* The tragedy of these inner vows was that when God wanted to save a Roman, He couldn't use the Christians in Antioch—their barnacles got in the way of their compassion. So He had to send people from Cyprus and Cyrene to share the Gospel with the Romans. The missionaries were sent to this barnacle-infested place to preach the right message—the Lord Jesus—to whoever would listen.

3. Jesus is preached in Antioch.

The believers at Antioch didn't preach on super-spiritual concepts that had no relevance to daily life. They just taught Christ—and they instilled such a wonder and awe for Him that people laid down their barnacles. They opened their hearts to the love and hope of the message, *and they found God again.*

Jesus has made it very clear that the only churches that will consistently grow and be effective in their mission to overthrow the enemy will be those that build on a constant, ongoing revelation of *who He is.* The church that overcomes and changes lives is the church that preaches Jesus.

For our churches to have any lasting relevance and fruit in our generation, we must preach Jesus—and not just on Sunday mornings. We must cultivate an atmosphere that celebrates the life, victory and presence of the Lord. We must preach Christ in our small groups and in our social functions—He must be present! We must consciously and consistently reveal Him—who He is, what He is like, what He desires to do for people and what His mission is.

According to our text, when we preach Jesus, *the hand of the Lord is with us and people turn* (see Acts 11:21). When we preach Jesus, barnacles come off, and broken people are healed.

4. Antioch Christians are encouragers.

An interesting feature to the story in Antioch is that when Christ was preached and people turned to Him, the leaders in Jerusalem sent a very peculiar minister to assist the work in Antioch. They didn't send Peter or James or John or any of the bigwig leaders—they sent Barnabas. They sent a man whose very name meant "Son of Encouragement" (Acts 4:36).

They must have reasoned that in this crucial stage in Antioch's development, they had to send the right gift. They must have waited on the Lord until someone spoke up and said, "I know who they need—they need Barnabas. There's a lot of brokenness in that city, and they need encouragement. Let's send Barnabas. Not only is he an encourager, but he's *the son of encouragement.* Encouragement flows through his veins. It's his spiritual DNA. Let's send Barnabas—that's what they need!"

The most important gift in Antioch is the gift of encouragement.

Acts 13 tells us that Barnabas was a prophet, but he wasn't sent to Antioch to prophesy—he was sent there to encourage the believers. He came alongside them and spoke words of life into their ears.

I like how he encouraged them. He encouraged them "with resolute heart to remain true to the Lord" (Acts 11:23). That's real encouragement! Encouragement is not just making others feel better; it's injecting courage into their veins so that they can remain steadfast to their calling. It's challenging them to stay true. It says, "You can do this! Remain true to the Lord—you can make it!"

5. Antioch Christians see grace.

Another feature of Barnabas' character that I like as much as his gift of encouragement is the fact that when he arrived at the church in Antioch, he "saw the evidence of the grace of God" (Acts 11:23, NIV). What do *you* see when you look at your church? Barnabas saw grace. He didn't see the barnacles—he saw the grace of God at work to lovingly scrape them away. He didn't see where the church lacked or was weak or needed to change—he saw what the church could become if it responded to grace.

We, the people of the church, *must* be people of grace if we are going to minister to barnacle-covered people who are looking for Jesus. I have to constantly check my heart to make sure that I am walking in grace. For example, when I see a couple that habitually struggles in their marriage, I have to search my heart to see if I am irritated by them or if true compassion flows through me.

I'm asking the Lord to let me see past the barnacles and into what He could accomplish if grace has its way. I want to "see grace." It's very easy to see a problem—anyone can do that. It doesn't require huge amounts of spiritual discernment to identify a problem or a weakness—but I want to see through the eyes of faith. I want to say, "You might be broken today, but that won't always be the case—someday you're going to preach to the nations!"

Send Barnabas to Antioch! He'll see past the barnacles into what believers can become if they keep preaching Jesus.

6. Antioch Christians invest in the next generation of leaders.

After Barnabas encouraged the people and imparted grace everywhere he went, he sent for Saul of Tarsus to help him in the ministry (see Acts 11:25–26). Barnabas had a heart for next-generation leaders, and he expressed it by inviting Saul to help him teach the people—a practice that they engaged in together for two solid years.

It wasn't the first time that Barnabas had reached out to Saul. He was the one who had seen a leader inside this former persecutor of the Church. He believed in Saul even when he was covered with barnacles and all of the other apostles were afraid of him. It was Barnabas who opened the door of favor for young Saul and injected courage and grace into him. Later, he did the same thing for a young man named John Mark, who initially had been an unreliable coward but eventually became an indispensable figure in the spread of the Gospel. Where would the world be today had Barnabas not pursued a young generation of leaders? Where will we be in our future if we don't do the same?

7. Antioch Christians touch the world.

When a relief effort needed to be launched for believers around the world, Antioch was the church to lead it. Antioch Christians have a heart for the nations.

What a great place! I love the Antioch church. I want to build one today. If we looked closely at the church in Antioch, we would see broken believers making their way to Jesus. We would see the message of Jesus Christ converting souls and healing barnacle-infested wounds. We would see the gift of encouragement changing the world. We would see grace—and we would see things the way God sees them. We would see the next generation of leaders in the Church. We would see the young apostle Paul studying in an Arabian desert, and we would see Barnabas knocking on his door and pulling him into the ministry. We would see amazing, wonderful things, but the most important thing we would see is *the world encountering Jesus like it never has before.*

I think you would fit in well in Antioch.

20

THE LIFE OF A PUZZLE PIECE

If Winter comes, can Spring be far behind?

Percy Bysshe Shelley

I pray thee, O God, that I may be beautiful within.

Socrates

*Our Creator would never have made such lovely days,
and have given us the deep hearts to enjoy them, above
and beyond all thought, unless we were meant to be
immortal.*

Nathaniel Hawthorne

Okay, so your church isn't Antioch. Or maybe it is, but you can't seem to find your niche in it. Let me share a few simple thoughts that might help.

Did you know that you and I are living inside a puzzle box?

Paul said that we have been "perfectly joined together" (1 Corinthians 1:10, NKJV). That phrase means "to organize and connect in a compact manner"—sort of like assembling a puzzle.

I've never been a huge puzzle fan. I've never had the patience, or the desire for that matter, to separate the corners from the straight edges and the random pieces. I doubt I've ever finished a jigsaw puzzle that had more than one hundred pieces in it. In fact, I think the only puzzle that I did enjoy was one that, when assembled, revealed a great picture of Han Solo and Chewbacca fighting stormtroopers. Other than that, I haven't had much interest in them.

Until lately.

I've been changing my tune ever since the Lord spoke to me through the *Parable of the Puzzle Piece*. Let's use our imaginations and evaluate several insights from this parable. I think it might help us understand why it can be so difficult to find our fit in the Body of Christ.

A puzzle piece is part of a puzzle.

Try not to let that profound revelation knock you over.

Webster defined the word *puzzle* as something that is "particularly baffling" and as a toy that "tests your ingenuity."[1] Puzzles are perplexing and bewildering, and they require a great degree of mental ingenuity to figure out. They're mysterious—just like our relationship with Jesus. Paul himself was baffled by the mystery of Christ (see Colossians 1:27). You and I are part of a mystery. We're part of a puzzle.

Life makes no sense to a puzzle piece until it realizes that it is part of a bigger picture.

If this is true for a puzzle piece, it is even more so for us: Our lives make no sense until we realize that we are part of a bigger story. We're a part of the picture of the Body of Christ that God has been painting since the foundation of time, and it's within this frame that our lives make sense.

Life makes no sense apart from God.

Without God, what does life consist of? We're born, we grow, we cultivate relationships, we work, we toil, we hope to experience a good life, and then we die. I understand the Preacher's lament in Ecclesiastes when he concluded that, apart from a relationship with God, life is vanity (see 1:2, 14; 2:11; 3:19; 12:8).

Life is miserable without a divine touch upon it. Life is futile without God.

We are a part of God's plan for the ages, and outside of this plan, life makes no sense.

Having recognized this fact, that life makes no sense for a puzzle piece until it realizes that it is part of a bigger picture, we must also recognize the next insight as true.

The individual puzzle piece often doesn't see the big picture.
Puzzle pieces spend a lot of time inside the box where it's dark and where they get jostled around, turned upside down and buried under other pieces. It's interesting to me that a puzzle piece can't take its place in the bigger picture until it gets *outside of the box.*

One of the young adults in our church recently had a dream in which Jesus hosted a party where He and each of the guests spent the evening exploding their boxes. We've got to get outside of the box! There's more to life than what we've been living—and we must let Him obliterate our boxes of limitation.

Even though the individual piece sometimes can't see the big picture, the next insight is still true.

The individual piece is a crucial part of the big picture.
Have you ever completed a puzzle only to find that you're missing one piece? What do you do when that happens? Do you say, "Oh, it's okay. I have *most* of the pieces"? More likely, you say, "Oh, no, it's ruined!" When a puzzle is miss-

ing even one piece, it appears incomplete—all you can see is the unfilled hole.

Every individual piece matters to the big picture—*just as you matter to God!* And you matter *to me.* And I'd better matter *to you.* We're family! We are not pawns in a cosmic chess match—we're crucial pieces of a beautiful picture that God Himself is creating.

The full beauty is never seen in an individual piece.

Not all pieces are beautiful; in fact, some pieces are downright ugly.

In my Star Wars puzzle from 1977, there was one piece that displayed only one thing on it—Han Solo's nostril. I hated that piece. As an individual piece, it was nothing but a close-up shot of Harrison Ford's nose hairs. It grossed me out—but it was still integral to the big picture. The picture would have been incomplete without it.

A lone puzzle piece will never fulfill its destiny.

A lone puzzle piece is not a puzzle in and of itself—it's a portrait. And God is not primarily interested in painting individual portraits; He's interested in a multicolored, multiethnic mosaic that will overthrow hell and establish His rule and reign on earth.

We are not portraits; we are puzzle pieces—*and we need each other.*

There's no stability in the puzzle until the pieces are connected.

Isn't this true? When the puzzle is "perfectly joined together," the entire thing can be picked up by one corner.

When my little sister was two years old, my dad had one of her photos turned into a puzzle. It was so much fun to watch her assemble a smiling picture of her own face. It certainly was the best puzzle I've ever seen. After it was completed, we applied clear glue to the surface, and it fused the pieces together until the individual parts became one *seamless* picture. That's God's goal for His Church—to take individuals and connect them together until they present a seamless glimpse of Jesus.

This next point is very important, but in reality, it can also be a little disheartening.

Sometimes it takes several attempts for the piece to find its fit.
Some puzzle pieces get overlooked for a long time, literally forgotten in the box. That's probably happened when you've assembled puzzles, hasn't it? You're almost done with the puzzle, and yet you're missing one or two pieces, so you look around and realize that they've been in the box the entire time. The whole time that the construction and assembling was occurring, these pieces lay, seemingly forgotten, inside the box. It sounds a little bit like the wilderness experience, doesn't it?

Have you ever tried to squeeze the wrong pieces together? If you try too hard, you'll bend the edges and damage the piece. It's better to wait until your space is ready for you than to try to squeeze yourself into a position that doesn't fit you. Wait for the spot that was custom-made for you. I hope you still believe it's out there.

Not only does it often take several attempts to find the right fit, but sometimes the Master picks up the same piece repeatedly *and then temporarily discards it* for another one. Have you ever been there? It can be a very dangerous place when we feel like we're constantly set aside. When we are in a season like this, it's imperative that we remind ourselves of the truth that *we are perfect for our God-given assignment.* God's niche for your life will fit you perfectly—our job is to seek Him until we discern and embrace it.

Sometimes your position won't be ready until other pieces are positioned properly.

God might be saving you for a special need!

Six years ago, the church I am currently serving didn't need me—there was no room for me. Six years ago, I felt set aside, discarded and tossed back into the box. Little did I know that God was assembling some pieces that would form a hole *and I would fit it perfectly!*

If you feel overlooked, turned upside down, buried inside a dark box or squeezed into a position that you know doesn't fit you—be encouraged! God has promised all through His Word to finish what He has begun. You fit into the big picture that He is forming, and He will eventually pick you up and plant you in a niche that only you can fill.

Let me conclude this little parable by offering a few more words of wisdom for puzzle pieces.

You do fit—but you must be patient.

A puzzle is assembled piece by piece, not all at once. Your time will come.

Use the seasons of waiting wisely.

I'm so glad that David killed Goliath—that story has encouraged me on a hundred different occasions. I'm not sure if he ever would have killed Goliath, though, if he hadn't been killing lions and bears first while he waited. Use the seasons of waiting wisely.

Master your piece of the puzzle.

Don't try to be a corner if you're a middle piece. Don't sneak to the center if you're a corner. If you're a straight edge, master the area you've been given. God gave you the gifts and personality you have because *the world needs you to be you.* So does the Church. Be the best, most Spirit-controlled *you* that you can be. We need you!

As frequently as possible, sneak a peak at the big picture.

The big picture brings us perspective and reminds us what we're all about. As I said earlier, *we are a part of God's plan for the ages.* By remembering this, we will ascend to a loftier view of our lives. We won't feel as if we're just toiling along with our work, our families and our faith. We'll soar like eagles as we realize we are contributing to the healing of a nation. We're not just changing diapers and loving teenagers—we're turning the tide in a generation that is desperate for a glimpse of the picture of Christ.

Don't get jealous of any other pieces—we're all equally important.

I know—everyone looks for the corner and border pieces first. That's okay. If you and I are center pieces, though, we're just as important as the edges that get a little more visibility and acclaim. God needs us. The world needs us. We carry a piece of His master plan for humanity—so let's carry it with pride.

Philippians 1:6 assures us that God is committed to getting us into the place that was made just for us. Let's commit not to jump ship in the process. Even if it takes a while to find our niche and to begin flourishing within it, let's hold steady and allow God to have His perfect way in us. Let it be said of us that after all of the highs and lows of our Christian lives, we "will still be praising" our Father (Psalm 84:4, NKJV).

Questions for Consideration and Application

1. Do you know that you are crucial for God's big-picture plan?

2. Have you identified your piece of the puzzle?

3. What are the "lions" and "bears" in your life that can be slain while you live the Parable of the Puzzle Piece?

4. When was the last time you glanced at the big picture?

21

OLD PEOPLE

I grow old learning something new every day.

Solon

To be seventy years young is sometimes far more cheerful and hopeful than to be forty years old.

Oliver Wendell Holmes

Rejoice, young man, during your childhood, and let your heart be pleasant during the days of young manhood. . . . Yet know that God will bring you to judgment for all these things.

Ecclesiastes 11:9

Sometimes I like to pretend that I'm very old and that I have wisdom far beyond my years. I like to try to view my life from the perspective of the grave looking back, because I think that if I can do that, I will live a life of greater impact and influence. When I was eighteen years old, I backpacked through Europe. While I was there I noticed that a number of the ancient cathedrals had been adorned with skulls in the artwork—it seems that the early Christian artisans also understood the truth that the grave is the best place to gain perspective on life.

Recently a number of young adults in our church hosted a very special banquet to honor the senior citizens of our congregation. We wanted to treat them to a night of honor and esteem that would send the clear message that we loved and needed them in our church. So we transformed our banquet hall into a 1940s dance club, we served them an elegant multiple-course meal, and we had a blast. We danced to music from the 1930s and 1940s, and we showed a PowerPoint presentation of pictures of these elderly saints from when they were teenagers. The room was decorated according to the historical themes of their lives, and we laughed and discussed trivia and memories from decades past. It was incredible!

As the evening progressed and the fun and games continued, I was deeply moved by the vast compilation of wisdom gathered in the room. I realized that there were many centuries' worth of marriage, child-rearing and life experience in front of us, so we took some time at the end of the night to ask these older believers to mentor us. They shared their pearls of truth and insight and exhorted our young people to love God, remain faithful to their families, find their callings and follow them dutifully. I prayed silently that the Lord would somehow imbed the truth of their words into the heart of each young person in the room. If the young adults would remember and practice those words, they would live better lives and be spared a myriad of grief and devastation. I love old people!

Let's apply the wisdom of the ages to the Church. If we were to view the Church from the grave looking back, what would we see? What would our final words of wisdom be if we were to speak to excited young Christians who were embarking on a lifetime of Christian service? Someday when

I'm an old man, I might have different advice, but today, pretending to be an old man, here is what I would say.

I'm not better than you.

I'm not better than you, and you aren't better than other Christians. We need to remember this because it's very easy to fall into the subtle pride that says that our vision or belief system is better than someone else's. Charismatics aren't better than Baptists, and Presbyterians aren't better than Lutherans. We're all brothers and sisters. We're family.

It's all about relationship.

Paul made an unforgettable point in his famous love chapter (see 1 Corinthians 13) when he wrote to the Corinthian believers that the grandest religious acts, if divorced from true love, are at best fingernails on a chalkboard. It's all about love, and it's all about relationship.

Be real.

I'm not perfect—and neither are you. In fact, it seems that the older I get, the more imperfect I become—either that or the more finicky God gets! Whether it's me backsliding or Him requiring more of me as I age, the obvious is true—I am a work in process, and any pretense otherwise is laughable. The world doesn't want a limp handshake and a cheesy smile—they want honesty and transparency; they want someone to cling to them and help them navigate the reality of life through the reality of knowing God.

Judge not.

We're going to need a lot of grace to make it through this adventure of life. Just maintaining a moral life in an immoral world requires grace. How much more does living a life that actually changes the world? Jesus reminded us that the merciful ones would receive a double portion of mercy.

We'll need it! Let's be living dispensers of mercy and grace versus judgment and criticism.

The prophet Zechariah revealed a great truth about the relationship between grace and the Holy Spirit. He said in an exhortation to Zerubbabel, who was trying to rebuild the broken temple of Jerusalem, that the work would be done "not by might nor by power" but by the Spirit of the Lord (Zechariah 4:6). He went on to say that mountains would fall and the top stone of the building would be brought forth with shouts of "Grace, grace to it!" (verse 7). Zechariah revealed that *grace is a medium through which the Holy Spirit likes to move.*

I love to preach on the virtues of humility, especially since James made it clear that *grace always follows humility* (see James 4:6). Humility releases grace, and grace attracts the Holy Spirit. Let's be humble carriers of grace, mercy and forgiveness. If we do this, we'll probably find that the power of the Holy Spirit is not far behind us.

In saying, "Don't judge," I'm not saying that we should be silent on the issues that grieve God's heart. Quite the reverse. The Church *must* oppose the things that oppose the Kingdom of God. We must heal the participants of abortion, but we must oppose the sin that has targeted an entire generation. We must love the individuals caught in gay lifestyles, but we must oppose the agenda that threatens to undermine God's plan for marriage and family. Jesus didn't tell us not to judge. He said to remember that the judgment we receive will be based on the way we dole it out to others throughout our lifetimes. If we will walk in grace, mercy and love, our judgments will be better received, and mercy will come back on our own heads. I once heard a pastor say, "If you're going to err, err on the side of mercy." I agree with him.

Don't forget the fallen.

Earlier in this book, I quoted Dr. Martin Luther King Jr. as saying that Jesus preached a "whosoever will, let him come" doctrine. Let's act on that thought and live our lives with open arms. Let's be a haven for weary travelers, and let's never forget our brethren who are struggling.

I heard a pastor share about a great man of God who had undergone some tragic situations that rocked his faith and confidence in the Lord. In his broken state, he had fallen into some serious sin. When this pastor heard of the plight of his hurting brother, he called a friend and said of the man, "It's our job to track him down!" That's what Jesus said of you and me, and that must be our posture if we ever want our lives to live up to our Sunday-morning claims. Don't forget the fallen—it's our job to track them down!

Don't neglect the mission.

Remember that the Christian faith doesn't make sense and it doesn't work apart from its mission. The entire destiny of mankind and the Christian faith was birthed out of God's passion to fill the earth with His glory and image. If we get too far removed from the passion for souls, or if we get too caught up in our secondary doctrines, we will find ourselves on a fast track toward disillusionment and burnout.

God will come through.

I love the verse in Psalm 37 in which David wrote, "I have been young and now I am old, yet I have not seen the righteous forsaken or his descendants begging bread" (verse 25). This is definitely an older person's perspective, because during many present-moment seasons in our lives, we can look at circumstances and easily question the faithfulness of God. We have to remember that we can't make eternal judgments based on the freeze-frames of our lives. God *will* come through. A younger generation of believers needs to hear this message as they settle into the trenches of 21st-century ministry.

God will come through. Maybe not in the way we imagine, and maybe not in the timing we would prefer, but He'll be there. It's His nature to come through. Paul wrote, "If we are faithless, He remains faithful, for He cannot deny Himself" (2 Timothy 2:13).

I love old people! Let's capitalize on the wisdom of the ages *today*, and let's follow our own sage advice.

22

THE ABUNDANT LIFE

Beyond this veil of tears, there is a life above;
Unmeasured by the flight of years, and all that life
is love.

James Montgomery

May you live all the days of your life.

Jonathan Swift

[Jesus said,] Be of good cheer; I have overcome the
world.

John 16:33, KJV

I think that the book of Ecclesiastes is probably one of the most overlooked and underrated books of the Bible, but it's probably one of the most important books in Scripture for those of us who are hungering for more out of life. Most of us know there is more, and we're in the relentless pursuit of it. We know that just attending church—or even being heavily involved in church activities—is not enough. Religious observances can't fulfill our deepest needs. There must still be more to life.

The book of Ecclesiastes is a giant "science project" in which a man, who has enough resources to test every theory under the sun, sets out in pursuit of the abundant life. He loves God, but he's convinced that there must be more to life than what he's been living. He's a lot like you and me—except that he's King Solomon, the wealthiest man on the planet, and he has the ability to pursue any and every whim his heart could desire.

For many, Ecclesiastes is a depressing book, because every few pages the writer laments that "all is vanity." But the honest truth is that for most of us, our best attempts at life have been vanity, too. So rather than dismissing Solomon's conclusions and then moving on to something easier, like the book of Psalms or the gospel of John, let's persevere and see what his experiment uncovers. He really does finally discover the pathway to true, abundant life. And we can find it, too.

It's interesting that Solomon begins his book by calling himself "the Preacher" (Ecclesiastes 1:1). In other words, he knew about God and religion, and he even had a position in that realm, but he still wasn't satisfied. So he set out in the pursuit of happiness—just like the Founding Fathers of our country did. The men who established the bedrock of our nation viewed the pursuit of happiness as an inalienable right. Solomon, too, felt it was his right to find a measure of happiness in life, so he went after it with all of the power that a king has at his disposal.

He started with good, clean fun, and then he moved on to the pleasures of alcohol and drugs. When these highs didn't quite satisfy, he tried the high of hard work. He built parks, gardens, vineyards, ponds and irrigation systems that watered entire forests. Although a career that is part of a balanced life is good and profitable, Solomon went overboard. He began to amass so much gold and silver that he became famous for his treasuries and bank accounts, but he still wasn't satisfied. Filled with an unsatisfied need, he moved on to darker addictions. He purchased multitudes of slaves and indulged in every lustful pleasure. An apt description of how far he took his pursuit of life is found in Ecclesiastes 2:10, in which Solomon wrote, "All that my eyes desired I did not refuse them. I did not withhold my heart from any pleasure." In other words, he tried it all.

Isn't it amazing, then, that his conclusion was that "all was vanity"? Let me give you the "CliffsNotes" to the results of his experiment, and you will see what the wisest man to ever walk the planet discovered about life. Amid all of his laments about the vanity and futility of life, he discovered the following things to be sources of both eternal value and temporal joy.

1. The perspective that this life is only a pilgrimage—a journey toward eternity

Solomon concluded that life on planet earth will make sense only if we realize that we are not ultimately destined to stay here. We are sojourners and pilgrims on our way to our eternal home, which, by the way, causes the greatest wonders that our current home can offer to pale in comparison. Hawaiian sunsets are but a child's crayon sketch compared to the brilliance of heaven's glow. The flashes of lightning over Pikes Peak on a brilliant Colorado night are mere flickers of beauty compared to the radiance of eternity. We are destined for more than what we're living, but some of that destiny will be realized only in the next life. I hope this isn't discouraging to you—Solomon didn't think it was. He thought it brought great perspective and contentment to know that all of this current reality, with its blessings and its woes, was a mere shadow of the glory that we will someday share.

2. Enjoyment of life's simple pleasures

Solomon concluded that it's not riches and wealth that bring the greatest source of contentment, but rather a heart of genuine gratitude. Someone who is able to enjoy a good cup of coffee under the stars as much as caviar in Manhattan knows how to savor life's simple pleasures and will find greater satisfaction as a result.

The classic business essay "Acres of Diamonds" emphasized this truth, as well. It related the story of a man who lost his wealth, health and life in pursuit of diamonds, only to discover that the mouth of the greatest diamond mine in Africa lay in the stream in his own backyard. It's okay to want more. I want more. I want to be blessed and prosperous and comfortable, but I also want to be content with what I have today. I want to savor the taste of the little things—like playing Barbies with my daughters and enjoying "couch time" with my wife after a long day of work.

3. True friendships

Solomon rightly concluded that a life lived alone is a vain and desperate thing. We are relational beings to our core. Because God birthed mankind out of His longing for a family, we will always be empty and discouraged if we aren't engaged in vibrant friendships. Even Jesus, who experienced long seasons of isolated prayer with His Father, never sent His disciples out alone. At the very least, they went out "two by two," so that, as Solomon said, they would have a good return for their labor and so that, if one fell, his companion would pull him up.

In his pursuit of life, Solomon saw a man with no son or brother and he said that, for that man, there was no end to his labor (see Ecclesiastes 4:8). The word *labor* that he used in that statement refers to the unfulfilled feeling of walking on a treadmill. He realized that some of the futility of our lives comes because we are trying to live our lives alone.

4. Humility and a teachable spirit before God

Solomon found that arrogance ends in ruin, while humility turns slaves into kings.

5. A good name

The power of a good name and the reward of a lasting legacy are things that can never be purchased, treasures that can never be lost. Solomon realized this and exhorted us to strive after them more than other fleeting trophies.

6. Employment in the area of one's giftedness

This is an important element of the abundant life, but it can be overwhelming to many people. The majority of us never reach that wonderful place where what we do best and most enjoy doing is also what we do the most often. Max Lucado has written a wonderful book called *The Cure for the Common Life*, in which he states that the greatest fulfillment in life comes from living in our "sweet spot"—that place where we do what we do best most often for the glory of God. When we are in this place, Solomon wrote, we tap into part of our natural reward from God—and true life ensues.

7. A balanced life

Solomon warned that a lack of balance in our lives would ruin us. The word *ruin* means "to grow numb, to be stunned and to become ravaged to the point of desolation and depopulation." A lack of balance will rob us of the very precious reserves of life that we're trying to build. A guest speaker in our church recently said, "A life of perpetual burnout is not a life that will be ready for the day of destiny." He went on to say that "there is enough time in every day to do the will of God for the day and keep the poetry alive in our soul."

8. The cultivation of an intimate, long-lasting marriage

If you are married, there are "acres of diamonds" awaiting you in your relationship with your spouse. They may need to be cultivated. They may be buried under some misunderstanding and boredom that needs to be washed away, but they're still there. Go after them! After pursuing a thousand women, Solomon concluded that the relationship with the wife of one's youth was where true happiness lay.

9. A genuine relationship with God

The famous conclusion of Solomon's little book says it all. He wrote, "The conclusion, when all has been heard, is: fear God and keep His commandments, because this applies to every person" (Ecclesiastes 12:13). I know that it may seem discouraging to think that after his all-encompassing quest for life, all Solomon concluded was that we should be afraid of God and make sure to keep the commandments. But that's not exactly what he was saying. Instead, he was saying this: If we will press into such a knowledge of God that our whole lives become enamored and enraptured with awe and respect for Him, and if we will do our best to live lives that please Him and make Him famous in the world, *then* we will have begun to tap into the heart of the matter and discover what true life is all about.

I've recently spent some time studying all of Jesus' references to the word *life*, and as I read the context surrounding each usage of the word, I discovered something very similar to Solomon's conclusion. Jesus seemed to think that the abundant life—the excessive, overflowing life of the Kingdom—comes to us through three primary sources:

1. A genuine, growing, passionate relationship with *Him*
2. Genuine, growing relationships with family and like-minded believers
3. Ministry in the area of our giftedness

When we're growing in our relationship with Him—not just logging time in endless church services—when we're living life with like-minded friends and family members and when we are bearing His image in an area that utilizes our gifts and passions, we will begin to discover some of what He meant when He said that He came so we could have life and "have it abundantly" (John 10:10). The word *abundantly* here means "exceeding the greatest abundance and overflowing in a super-abundant way." I'm ready for a super-abundant overflow of life. How about you?

Questions for Consideration and Application

1. What significant relationships has the Lord given you to help you experience true life?

2. Are you investing adequately in these relationships?

3. Are you guarding the power of your good name?

4. Are you ministering in the area of your gifts?

5. Do you ever consider the fact that this life here on earth is merely the dress rehearsal for your eternal life in heaven with Jesus? How does this change your attitude and perspective?

23

SLEEPING WITH BATHSHEBA ... AGAIN

*Every day is a birthday, for every day we are born
anew.*

Ellen Browning Scripps

*When the Light of Life falls upon the life of men, secret
powers begin to unfold, sleeping perceptions begin to
awake, and the whole being becomes alive unto God.*

John Henry Jowett

So, now what? We've looked at the good, the bad and
the ugly of church life, and we've recognized that, for
all of its very human shortcomings, the Church is still the
Bride and the Body of Christ. He is still as committed as
ever to building it into a force that will overthrow hell in
every region of society. We have also learned that we can't
speak of the Church in the third person, because *we* are
the Church. We can no more divorce ourselves from it than
our bodies could divorce themselves from our lungs and
expect to keep on breathing. I'm certainly not saying that

we have to settle for church as it has always been done— far from it. I'm like you—I'm finished with religion that helps only the ultra-disciplined but offers no life for hurting, desperate people. I'm done with church politics that consume precious hours of our lives but bear no eternal fruit. I'm done with irrelevance and self-centered, shallow church experiences.

But I'm not done with the Church.

I might be a separatist who seeks to found a better place of religious freedom or I might be a puritan who strives to bring change from within, but I am still the Church. And when Jesus returns to sweep His Bride off of her feet, I want to be one of the ones He asks to dance. I want to have a track record of unquenchable devotion, unwavering fidelity and the constant championing of the role of the Church in society. I agree with Jack Hayford that we are entering the age of the Church. We, the people of God, are not going to be relegated to the sidelines of a cultural maelstrom, but we will again take our place as salt and light and achieve a degree of excellence that draws the world to Christ.

Jesus said He would help us do it. That gives us pretty good odds—as long as we don't quit.

Let me wrap up our time together with a final thought. Have you ever considered the fact that, although David smeared his good reputation with his adulterous relationship with Bathsheba, there came a time when the Lord told him to sleep with her again? Their first child, the product of their sin, died and entered heaven to be with the Lord (a blessing for the child, but a punishment for David). On the heels of the tragic news, David arose, washed his face, changed his clothes and entered the house of the Lord to worship. After worshiping the Lord amid his grief, the Bible tells us that David went in to Bathsheba, comforted her and slept with her . . . again (see 2 Samuel 12:24). This time the fruit of their relationship was the child Solomon, and God loved this little boy so much that He sent a prophet to his parents to tell them as much.

I can't imagine that David and Bathsheba's second time in bed together was very romantic. It was probably awkward and maybe even a little shameful, but David was asked to do it—because there was still life in Bathsheba, and God wanted to take their tragic situation and bring something good out of it.

Perhaps there's a Bathsheba waiting for you. Perhaps there are relationships in your church that ended in pain, and you've vowed never to return to them. Perhaps you've written your church off as an irrelevant, hurtful institution, and you have no intention of ever giving it a second chance. I'm not telling you that you have to engage in a hurtful situation again—I don't know if you should attempt another try at reconciliation or not. But God knows, and He has a word for you if you'll ask Him.

God is looking for 21st-century Christians who will build His 21st-century Church in such a way that the world sees the glory of God and runs to be reconciled to Him. He is looking for sons and daughters who will be "ten times better" than the world and will bear His image well in their corner of it. He is looking for people who will move from woundedness to brokenness, people with whom He can share His anointing to change the culture and usher in a great modern-day move of God. In other words, He's looking for you.

He knew that Bathsheba was carrying a king inside of her, and He knows that, despite its flaws and failures, the Church is still His plan to win the world. There might be life left in her still.

I'm convinced of it . . . because *there's life left in you, and you are the Church!*

**Questions for Consideration
and Application**

1. Are there any relationships that you need to revisit?

2. Have you sworn off of any practices out of your hurt? Which ones
   might you need to revisit?

3. Do you believe that there is still life left in you?

Notes

Chapter 5: Troubled Waters

1. George Barna, *Revolution* (Wheaton, Ill.: Tyndale House Publishers, 2005), 14.

Chapter 10: Your Pastor

1. Dutch Sheets and Chris Jackson, *Second in Command: Strengthening Leaders Who Serve Leaders* (Shippensburg, Pa.: Destiny Image, 2005), 130–31.
2. Ibid., 111–12.
3. Ibid., 123–24.
4. Gene Edwards, *A Tale of Three Kings* (Wheaton, Ill.: Tyndale House Publishers, 1980, 1992), 27–28.

Chapter 13: A Leader Who Lost His Cutting Edge

1. Warren Baker and Eugene Carpenter, *The Complete Word Study Dictionary, Old Testament* (Chattanooga, Tenn.: AMG Publishers, 2003), #5387.

Chapter 16: Ten Times Better

1. *The Key Word Study Bible* (Chattanooga, Tenn.: AMG Publishers, 1990), #1935.
2. John Eldredge, *Waking the Dead* (Nashville, Tenn.: Thomas Nelson Publishers, 2003), 87.
3. Winston Churchill, "Their Finest Hour," www.winstonchurchill.org.

Chapter 18: The 21st-Century Christian

1. From George Barna's website, www.barna.org, accessed May 30, 2005.

Chapter 19: The 21st-Century Church

1. Frank Damazio, *The Gate Church* (Portland, Ore.: City Bible Publishing, 2000), 15–16.

2. *The Key Word Study Bible*, #5537.

3. Ibid., #2347.

Chapter 20: The Life of a Puzzle Piece

1. See www.websters-online-dictionary.org/definition/puzzle.

Chris Jackson is a pastor with a passion to see believers blossom into their fullest potential in Christ. He has served as the executive pastor at Freedom Church in Colorado Springs, Colorado (under senior pastor Dutch Sheets, formerly Springs Harvest Fellowship), since 2000. He is a dynamic communicator who presents biblical truth in a fresh, insightful and relevant way. Pastor Chris and Jessica Jackson moved to Colorado Springs from Washington State, where they had been on staff and ministered for several years with the Master's Commission, a dynamic school of ministry for young adults. Their greatest longing is to see believers made whole and walking in their God-given destinies. They have two beautiful daughters, Amber and Madelyn. Chris is the coauthor of two books with Pastor Dutch Sheets: *Praying through Sorrows* and *Second in Command: Strengthening Leaders Who Serve Leaders*. To contact Chris, email him at christen-jackson@hotmail.com.